国际经济与贸易系列规划教材

外刊导读

Guide to Reading of Foreign Journals

崔艳娟　罗鹏　金南顺　编著

大连理工大学出版社

内容提要:本书充分体现导读的作用,文章选自国际知名报刊,通过对文章的分析,介绍国际最新资讯,介绍英文刊物的阅读方法。所选文章涵盖的范围包括:经济、贸易、营销、管理、财政、投资、科技、政治、恐怖主义、社会生活、环境、健康等。

图书在版编目(CIP)数据

外刊导读 : 汉英对照 / 崔艳娟,罗鹏,金南顺编著
-- 大连 : 大连理工大学出版社,2010.3
(国际经济与贸易系列规划教材)
ISBN 978-7-5611-5421-2

Ⅰ. ①外… Ⅱ. ①崔… ②罗… ③金… Ⅲ. ①对外贸易-英语-阅读教学-高等学校-教材 Ⅳ. ①H319.4

中国版本图书馆 CIP 数据核字(2010)第 031546 号

大连理工大学出版社出版

地址:大连市软件园路 80 号 邮政编码:116023
发行:0411-84708842 邮购:0411-84703636 传真:0411-84701466
E-mail:dutp@dutp.cn URL:http://www.dutp.cn

大连美跃彩色印刷有限公司印刷 大连理工大学出版社发行

幅面尺寸:170mm×240mm 印张:9.5 字数:175 千字
2010 年 3 月第 1 版 2010 年 3 月第 1 次印刷

责任编辑:汪会武 邵 婉 责任校对:千 川
封面设计:波 朗

ISBN 978-7-5611-5421-2 **定 价:18.00 元**

前言 Foreword

随着国际化进程的加剧，人才市场对于高校专业教育提出了更高的要求，即不仅要具有扎实的专业功底，还要保持对外界信息的适时知晓。呈现在读者面前的这本《外刊导读》一书正是为了满足上述要求而精心编撰的。本书可用做专业教材，亦可用于社会各界人士的参考阅读书目。

本书在编写中突出了以下特点：

第一，充分体现了"导读"的作用。本书给出了阅读英文报刊的基本常识、阅读技巧以及常用外刊网站(附录)，重在引导学生学会阅读英文报刊等材料，从而充分利用其中的信息进行科学研究。

第二，文章选取上的专业性与时事性。本书在文章的选取上，除了体现专业性(在前12个单元中财经类文章有5个单元)，还注重时事性，所选取的文章都是近期世界范围内经济、政治、社会生活等领域的最新焦点问题，并计划进行后续版的编写，以随时跟踪国内外经贸、政治领域的热点和焦点问题，为读者提供最新的资讯。

第三，文章来源的权威性。本书中每一篇文章均从国际知名的英文报刊杂志中选取，包括美国的《纽约时报》、《华盛顿邮报》、《洛杉矶时报》、《华尔街日报》、《今日美国》、《芝加哥论坛报》、《纽约每日新闻》、《纽约邮报》、《财富》、《时代》、《福布斯》、《读者文摘》，英国的《泰晤士报》、《金融时报》、《每日镜报》、《每日快报》、《观察家报》、《经济学家》等。保证了文章的权威性。

全书共13个单元。1～12单元，分别为：全球经济、国际金融、投资、管理、营销战略、现代技术、现代科学、世界政治、恐怖主义、社会生活、世界环境以及人类健康。每个单元第一篇文章前有背景资料介绍，以便读者更好地理解正文；文章后提供了难点解释(正文中以数字顺序标出)以及精华长句(正文中以黑体标出)、专题讨论和练习题等,以巩固对文章内容的理解与掌握。每个单元的第二篇文章则是未做任何注释的原文,作为扩展阅读,从而提高阅读理解能力。每篇文章语言表达精炼,词汇丰富,知识性强,观点明确,同时在一定程度上体现了趣味性。第13单元介绍了英文报刊的特点以及相关的阅读技巧,以提高读者对于本书以及其他外刊的阅读能力。最后,附录给出了常用的外刊网站资源。

本书是集体智慧的成果,是由大连工业大学教师崔艳娟(第2、4、6、7、8单元),大连大学教师罗鹏(第1、3、5、13单元)和大连大学金南顺教授(第9、10、11、12单元)共同完成的,其中罗鹏做了大量的资料搜集和整理工作。大连大学经济管理学院硕士研究生陈丕方、吕园园、潘礼尧、范肇洲、周春丽等也做了大量基础性的工作。

本书的完成得益于所有撰稿人的奉献,但由于水平所限,难免存在缺陷和不当之处,敬请专家、学者和广大读者给与批评与指正,我们将不胜感激。

此外,本书在编写过程中参考了大量的图书文献等资料,并借鉴和引用了有关的研究成果,有的在书中列了出来,有的由于统计的原因可能没有列出,在此谨向所有有关图书文献的作者表示衷心的感谢。

崔艳娟　罗鹏　金南顺

2010年1月于大连

Contents 目录

UNIT 1 GLOBAL ECONOMY ······ 1
Text: Global Fears of a Recession Grow Stronger ······ 2
Extensive Reading: The U.S. Financial Crisis Is Spreading to Europe ······ 9
UNIT 2 INTERNATIONAL FINANCE ······ 14
Text: Deals That Were Doomed from the Start: A Look Back ······ 15
Extensive Reading: Mailing Our Way to Solvency ······ 23
UNIT 3 INVESTMENT ······ 26
Text: New Regulations Sure to Accompany Bailout ······ 27
Extensive Reading: Global Stocks: Should You Pull Out? ······ 34
UNIT 4 MANAGEMENT ······ 38
Text: Up From the Rubble: Post-Recession Planning ······ 39
Extensive Reading: Why limiting CEO Pay is a Good Idea ······ 47
UNIT 5 MARKETING STRATEGY ······ 50
Text: How Small Stores Can Lure Holiday Shoppers ······ 51
Extensive Reading: Small Name in TVs Has Big Plans ······ 57
UNIT 6 MODERN TECHNOLOGY ······ 59
Text: A Home Network Where Your TV Talks to Your Fridge ······ 60
Extensive Reading: Using Video Games as Bait to Hook Readers ······ 68
UNIT 7 MODERN SCIENCE ······ 74
Text: China Launches Space walk Mission ······ 75
Extensive Reading: Mars Weather Forecast: Snow ······ 82
UNIT 8 WORLD POLITICS ······ 84
Text: Mistrust and Hostility Between Two Koreas Shapes Life on an Island ······ 86

Extensive Reading: Envoy Pushes to Save Deal on Disarming North Korea ······ 93

UNIT 9 TERRORISM ······ 95

Text: Confronting Taliban, Pakistan Finds Itself at War ······ 96

Extensive Reading: Terrorists and Spies, Weaving Their Webs ······ 102

UNIT 10 SOCIAL LIFE ······ 106

Text: In 'Sweetie' and 'Dear', a Hurt for the Elderly ······ 107

Extensive Reading: Animal restaurant in Los Angeles ······ 112

UNIT 11 WORLD ENVIRONMENT ······ 117

Text: New Coast Guard Task in Arctic's Warming Seas ······ 118

Extensive Reading: The Top 20 Effects of Global warming ······ 124

UNIT 12 HEALTH ······ 128

Text: Are Bad Times Healthy? ······ 129

Extensive Reading: Fan in Room Seems to Cut Infants' Risk of Crib Death ······ 134

UNIT 13 LANGUAGE FEATURES ······ 136

附录 外刊网址 ······ 145

第 1 章
UNIT 1
GLOBAL ECONOMY

• Text •

背景参考

目前，由于美国金融危机导致的全球性金融危机，已成为全世界关注的大事。这场金融危机不但大大震荡了美国的经济，而且也危及到包括中国在内的世界主要发达国家与发展中国家，并且已经对全球经济产生了重大的负面影响。全球经济一体化下，各国政治经济联系密切，美国的金融危机迅速席卷全球，演变为全球性金融危机。

此次金融危机，由 2008 年美国爆发的“次贷危机”扩大而来。所谓次贷危机，即次级抵押贷款危机，这其中主要包括次级购房贷款。“次贷”即指给那些不符合抵押贷款市场标准的借款者也提供按揭服务。“次贷危机”始于美国房地产市场。其核心问题与危机的起源，就是凭借按揭贷款而购买了房子的人，大规模发生了“断供”现象，即无力继续偿付每月的贷款及利息，致使放贷银行长年积累的大规模的不良资产日益增多，直至烂账太多而接连发生破产。

事实上，早在 2007 年 4 月，美国第二大次级房贷公司 —— 新世纪金融公司的破产就暴露了次级抵押债券的风险。从 2007 年 8 月开始，美联储做出反应，向金融体系注入流动性资金以增加市场信心，美国股市也得以在高位维持。然而，2008 年 8 月，美国房贷两大巨头 —— 房利美和房地美股价暴跌，持有“两房”债券的金融机构大面积亏损。美国财政部和美联储被迫接管“两房”，以表明政府应对危机的决心。但接踵而来的是：总资产高达 1.5 万亿美元的世界两大顶级投资银行雷曼兄弟和美林相继爆出问题，前者被迫申请破产保护，后者被美国银行收购；总资产高达1万亿美元的全球最大保险商——美国国际集团(AIG)也难以为继；美国政府在选择接管AIG以稳定市场的同时却对其他金融机构“爱莫能助”。由此可以看出，美国政府不当的房地产金融政策为危机埋下了伏笔。同时，金融衍生品的“滥用”，拉长了金融交易链条，助长了投机，再加上美国货币政策推波助澜。本次美国金融危机由次贷危机引发，追究深层次原因则是美国长期超前消费的经济模式造成的。

面对这气势汹汹的金融危机风暴，美国政府不得不全力进行抵抗，由政府出资予以救市，使那些受到次贷危机风暴威胁而摇摇欲坠的、有影响的金融企业与银行免遭破产，避免金融界出现破产的多米诺骨牌效应，以稳定美国的金融运作秩序，及时在金融危机与实体经济之间构筑保护性防火墙。

Global Fears of a Recession Grow Stronger

By MARK LANDLER

Published: *October* 6, 2008

World Business Column of The New York Times

When the White House brought out its $700 billion rescue plan two weeks ago, its sheer size was meant to soothe the global financial system, restoring trust and confidence. Three days after the plan was approved, it looks like a pebble tossed into the sea.

The crisis that began as a made-in-America subprime lending problem[1] and radiated across the world is now circling back home, where it pummeled stock and credit markets on Monday.

While the Bush administration's bailout package offers help to foreign banks, it seems to have done little to reassure investors, particularly in Europe, where banks are failing and countries are racing to stave off panicky withdrawals after first playing down the depth of the crisis.

Far from being the cure for the world's ills, economists said, the rescue plan

might end up being a stopgap[2] for the United States alone. With Europe showing few signs of developing a coordinated response to the crisis, there is very little on the horizon to calm rattled investors.

The vertiginous drop in stock markets on both sides of the Atlantic on Monday reflected not only those fears but also a growing belief that the crisis could tip the world into a global recession.

Indeed, the ripple effects from Europe and the United States were amplified as they spread to stock markets in Russia, Brazil, Indonesia and the Middle East. These countries had little to do with the subprime crisis but were vulnerable[3] to a sudden halt in the flow of money. They lack even the veneer[4] of national or regional cooperation that protects Europe and the United States. Stock markets in emerging economies recorded their worst one-day decline in 21 years on Monday, with trading in Russia and Brazil halted to stem an investor panic.[5]

"It looks pretty ugly down the road," said Simon Johnson, an economist at the Massachusetts Institute of Technology and a former chief economist of the International Monetary Fund who specializes in financial crises. "Everybody is going to get caught up in this."

The global nature of the crisis and its growing collateral damage ought to galvanize countries to work together to fashion a concerted response[6], Mr. Johnson said. There is a chance to do that this week, with dozens of finance ministers and central bankers converging on Washington for the annual meetings of the I. M. F. and the World Bank.

The trouble is, these institutions no longer have the resources or authority to lead such an effort. The I. M. F., which played a central role in the Asian crisis, has been relegated to the sidelines this time — its credibility tarnished by that episode and its skills ill-suited to a crisis in advanced economies. These days, it mainly issues lonely warnings about the impact on developing countries.

The Group of 7[7], which once functioned as a sort of command center for the global economy, is similarly depleted, according to critics. It no longer represents the world's economic drivers, they said, and badly needs to be expanded to include rising powers like China and India.

"The globalization of the crisis means we need a globalization of responses," said C. Fred Bergsten, the director of the Peterson Institute for International Economics. "But most of the responses will be national. For all the institutions we have, we don't have the right institutions to do this."

That is particularly true in Europe, which has an effective central bank but lacks a unified legislature or treasury to coordinate or finance a rescue of the banking system. So far, economists say, Europe's response to the crisis in its banks has been mostly marked by denial and dissension.

From London to Berlin, governments are clinging to a piecemeal approach. The British and the Germans have resisted a broader solution, because they fear they will end up rescuing their neighbors.

A weekend meeting of European leaders in Paris, called by President Nicolas Sarkozy, ended with a pledge that Europe would not countenance a bank failure like that of Lehman Brothers, but little else.

Part of the problem is the nature of this crisis: bailouts of banks are costly and unpopular with taxpayers — even more so, as in Europe, where burden sharing is a perennial[8] sore point.

"Taxpayers won't agree to bail out the banking system of other countries," said Thomas Mayer, the chief European economist at Deutsche Bank in London. "Not even in Europe, where you have a neutral framework, could you get people to cooperate on a joint effort."

As the problems in Europe have worsened, the crisis has taken on an "every country for itself" quality. When Ireland placed a guarantee on all bank deposits and debt last week, it angered neighbors, who feared capital would flee their banks to the safer haven of Dublin. Now, Germany, Sweden, Denmark and Austria have all pledged to guarantee deposits.

"If you do this one by one, it destabilizes people's deposits in other countries," Mr. Johnson said. "It's mind-boggling[9] that the Europeans have coordinated so little up until this point."

With Europe and the United States deep in crisis, economists said, the rest of the world could not help but suffer. Robert B. Zoellick, the president of the World Bank, warned that the crisis could be a "tipping point" for the developing world.

"A drop in exports, as well as capital inflow, will trigger a falloff in investments," Mr. Zoellick said in a speech on Monday. "Deceleration of growth and deteriorating financial conditions, combined with monetary tightening, will trigger business failures and possibly banking emergencies."

The immediate danger, economists say, are countries in Eastern and Central Europe, like Bulgaria and Estonia, which run steep trade deficits and are vulnerable to a sudden flight of foreign capital.

Iceland, with an overheated economy and suffocating foreign debt, may prove to be the first national casualty of the crisis. On Monday, threatened by a wholesale financial collapse, the government in Reykjavik assumed sweeping powers to intervene in its banking industry.

"We were faced with the real possibility that the national economy would be sucked into the global banking swell and end in national bankruptcy," Prime Minister Geir H. Haarde said on Monday.

But with global growth slowing sharply, the problems could spread to larger emerging markets, even China, which has a hefty current account surplus and immense foreign reserves.

"Where is China going to sell its exports?" Mr. Johnson of M. I. T. said. "Everyone is going into recession at the same time."

This week, the focus will be on the Group of 7, whose finance ministers and central bankers are scheduled to meet on Friday at the Treasury Department. The group issued a perfunctory statement of support for the United States, after the Treasury secretary, Henry M. Paulson Jr., briefed members about the rescue plan in a conference call two weeks ago.

But European finance ministers, notably Peer Steinbrück of Germany, noted that the crisis began in the United States, and played down the need for a systemic European response.

Mr. Zoellick, in his speech, said flatly that the Group of 7 "is not working." He advocates expanding the group — which includes the United States, Canada, Britain, Italy, France, Germany and Japan — to include emerging economies like Brazil, China, India and Saudi Arabia.

The urgency of the moment, experts said, demands a bolder response from the Group of 7. Mr. Bergsten said the group should commit to a coordinated stimulus plan[10] to stave off a recession.

"Just as the U.S. rescue plan may not be enough," he said, "a U.S. stimulus plan by itself will not be enough."

难点注释

1 subprime lending problem 次级抵押贷款问题

即指一些贷款机构向信用程度较差和收入不高的借款人提供的贷款。在美国住房市场高度繁荣时，次级抵押贷款市场迅速发展。但随着美国住房市场大幅降温，加上利率上升，很多次级抵押贷款市场的借款人无法按期偿还借款，导致一些放贷机构遭受严重损失甚至破产。美国抵押贷款市场的"次级"(Subprime)及"优惠级"(Prime)是以借款人的信用条件作为划分界限的。根据信用的高低，放贷机构对借款人区别对待，从而形成了两个层次的市场。信用低的人申请不到优惠贷款，只能在次级市场寻求贷款。两个层次的市场服务对象均为贷款购房者，但次级市场的贷款利率通常比优惠级抵押贷款利率高2%～3%。

Subprime lending (near-prime, non-prime, or second-chance lending) in finance means making loans that are in the riskiest category of consumer loans and are typically sold in a market from prime loans. The standards for determining risk categories refer to the size of the loan, "traditional" or "nontraditional" structure of the loan, borrower credit rating, ratio of borrower debt to income or assets, ratio of loan to value or collateral, documentation provided on those loans which do not meet Fannie Mae or Freddie Mac underwriting guidelines for prime mortgages (are "non-conforming"). Although there is no single, standard definition, in the United States subprime loans are usually classified as those where the borrower has an FICO score below 640. Subprime lending encompasses a variety of credit types, including morgages, auto loans, and credit cards. The term was popularized by the media during the "credit crunch" of 2007. (*http://en.wikipedia.org/wiki/Subprime_lending*)

2 stopgap 权宜之计

something contrived to meet an urgent need or emergency

3 vulnerable 脆弱的，敏感的

capable of being wounded; susceptible of wounds or external injuries

4 veneer 虚假的外表，虚饰

an ornamental coating to a building consisting of a thin layer of superior wood glued to a base of inferior wood

5 Stock markets in emerging economies recorded their worst one-day decline in 21 years on Monday, with trading in Russia and Brazil halted to stem an investor panic.

新兴经济体国家的股票市场在本周一突破了记录，达到了 21 年来的单日最大跌幅，同时在俄罗斯及巴西的贸易也暂停下来以遏制出现的投资恐慌。

6 The global nature of the crisis and its growing collateral damage ought to galvanize countries to work together to fashion a concerted response.

全球性危机的本质以及它所带来的相关危害应该唤起各国的共同努力，以制定一个协调一致的对策。

7 The Group of 7 七国集团

20 世纪 70 年代，主要资本主义国家的经济形势一度恶化，接连发生的美元危机、石油危机、布雷顿森林体系瓦解和严重的经济危机把西方国家弄得焦头烂额。为共同解决世界经济和货币危机，协调经济政策，重振西方经济，1975 年 7 月初，法国首先倡议召开由法国、美国、日本、英国和西德五国参加的最高级首脑会议。意大利及加拿大后来加入。此后由这七个主要西方工业国家参加的最高级首脑会议通称为西方七国集团首脑会议。

The Group of 7, also known as the G7 or G-7, is the meeting of the finance ministers from a group of seven industrialized nations. It was formed in 1976, when Canada joined the Group of Six: France, Germany, Italy, Japan, United Kingdom, and United States. The finance ministers of these countries meet several times a year to discuss economic policies. Their work is supported by regular, functional meetings of officials, including the G7 Finance Deputies. (*http://en.wikipedia.org/wiki/G7*)

8 perennial 长期的，经常出现的

continuing without cessation or intermission; perpetual; unceasing; never failing

9 mind-boggling 令人难以置信的

10 stimulus plan 刺激(经济的)计划

Stimulus plan is a term used to deal a situation where the government changes its fiscal policy of spending and taxation in order to bolster and revive an economy that is in a recession. By spending money on state and federal infrastructure, the government hopes to provide jobs, and jump-start the failing economy.

(*http://www.yourdictionary.com/define-economic-stimulus.html*)

精华长句

1 While the Bush administration's bailout package offers help to foreign banks, it seems to have done little to reassure investors, particularly in Europe, where banks are failing and countries are racing to stave off panicky withdrawals after first playing down the depth of the crisis.

虽然布什政府的一揽子救市措施对外资银行提供帮助,但似乎并没有安抚投资者,特别是在欧洲:那里的银行正在破产,各国先是淡化这场危机的严重性,现在则纷纷紧急规避恐慌性提款。

2 Far from being the cure for the world's ills, economists said, the rescue plan might end up being a stopgap for the United States alone. With Europe showing few signs of developing a coordinated response to the crisis, there is very little on the horizon to calm rattled investors.

经济学家说,拯救计划可能最终只是针对美国的一个权宜之计,远远无法解决全世界的问题。几乎没有迹象显示欧洲各国会采取协调一致的应对危机的措施,因此没有办法使得慌乱的投资者平静下来。

3 From London to Berlin, governments are clinging to a piecemeal approach. The British and the Germans have resisted a broader solution, because they fear they will end up rescuing their neighbors.

从伦敦到柏林,政府都采用化整为零、零敲碎打的办法。英国和德国已经抵制了更广泛的解决方案,因为他们担心最终会拯救他们的邻国。

4 "A drop in exports, as well as capital inflow, will trigger a falloff in investments," Mr. Zoellick said in a speech on Monday. "Deceleration of growth and deteriorating financial conditions, combined with monetary

tightening, will trigger business failures and possibly banking emergencies."

"出口下降以及资本流入,将会引发投资下降,"佐利克在星期一的一次讲话中说。"经济增长减速和日益恶化的财务状况,再加上紧缩货币政策,将引发企业倒闭以及银行出现紧急情况。"

5 But with global growth slowing sharply, the problems could spread to larger emerging markets, even China, which has a hefty current account surplus and immense foreign reserves.

但随着全球经济增长的急剧放缓,问题可能会蔓延到一些主要的新兴市场,甚至是有着巨额的经常账户余额以及巨大外汇储备的中国。

6 This week, the focus will be on the Group of 7, whose finance ministers and central bankers are scheduled to meet on Friday at the Treasury Department. The group issued a perfunctory statement of support for the United States, after the Treasury secretary, Henry M. Paulson Jr., briefed members about the rescue plan in a conference call two weeks ago.

本星期的焦点是七国集团的财政部长和中央银行行长计划于本周五在财政部会面。两星期前,在一次电话会议上,财政部长亨利·保尔森简要介绍了救援计划。此后七国发表了一份敷衍了事支持美国的声明。

讨论

1 What are the root causes of the Global Financial Crisis?

2 What are the impacts of the Global Financial Crisis on the economy of the world as well as China?

3 What are the countermeasures to the Global Financial Crisis?

• Extensive Reading •

The U.S. Financial Crisis Is Spreading to Europe

By MARK LANDLER

Published: *September* 30, 2008

World Business Column of The New York Times

WASHINGTON — Barely a week after Europeans rebuffed American pleas to join in their bailout of the banking system, Europe now faces a financial crisis almost as grave as that in the United States — demonstrating how swiftly this contagion is spreading around the world.

In the last two days, governments from London to Berlin have seized or bailed out five faltering banks. In Ireland, where rumors of panicked withdrawals from banks spooked the stock market, the government has offered a two-year blanket guarantee on all deposits and bank debt.

Asia has been less buffeted by the turmoil, though a brief run on a bank in Hong Kong last week brought back dark memories of June 1997, when speculation against the Thai currency sparked a financial crisis that fanned rapidly across Asia, and later to Brazil and Russia.

Economists see a parallel between these two crises a decade apart: once creditors panic and begin to pull out their holdings, the underlying health of banks — or entire countries — no longer matters a great deal. In a global financial system, national borders are porous.

"In this day and age, a bank run spreads around the world, not around the block," said Thomas Mayer, the chief European economist at Deutsche Bank. "Once a bank run is under way, it doesn't matter anymore if you have good loans or bad loans. People lose confidence in you."

In a sign of how vulnerable Russia remains to contagion, officials halted trading on the Moscow stock exchange for two hours on Tuesday morning, fearing investor reaction to the House's rejection of the Bush administration's bailout plan. Trading resumed, and after President Bush vowed to win approval of the package, shares bounced back.

"People ask, 'What on earth is happening with Russia?'" said Roland Nash, chief analyst at Renaissance Bank in Moscow. "Russia is reacting to the unprecedented size, complexity and danger coming out of the U. S."

The shock waves could reverberate to the United States, experts said, since

Russia has plowed its oil wealth into American debt, including Fannie Mae's. Russia has additional problems, including unstable oil prices and a newly assertive foreign policy that is unpopular with many investors.

The trigger for the loss of confidence in Europe, Mr. Mayer and other experts said, was the Treasury Department's decision two weeks ago to let Lehman Brothers fail. That ricocheted through European markets, hurting banks and retail investors with exposure to Lehman.

It took a few days longer for Europeans to digest the implications of the collapse. But now that they have, they are turning a remorseless eye on other institutions they suspect of being vulnerable.

As the White House scrambles to retool its rescue plan for the financial system, the global creep of the crisis has far-reaching implications, administration officials and outside experts said.

It is likely to move Europeans to mount a more coordinated effort to shore up banks, a move that the Treasury secretary, Henry M. Paulson Jr., pleaded for last week. President Nicolas Sarkozy of France is calling for a mini-summit of leaders in Paris on Friday.

"We all agree that the method by which everyone comes up with ad hoc solutions in his corner the moment a crisis starts in a financial company isn't a systematic enough method," said Prime Minister Jean-Claude Juncker of Luxembourg, chairman of a group of European finance officials.

On Tuesday, France and Belgium threw a $9 billion lifeline to Dexia, a Belgian-French lender — a day after Belgium, the Netherlands, and Luxembourg cobbled together $16.2 billion to rescue another bank, Fortis.

Europe's woes could place additional burdens on an American plan, as more banks fall into distress. If the Treasury wins Congressional approval to buy mortgage-related securities from banks, how it prices those assets will affect the solvency of European institutions.

Some of these banks suffer a form of guilt by association by being in the home lending business. Others, like Fortis, lack a strong base of deposits, which acts as a buffer against credit-related jitters.

Countries that suffered housing bubbles — like Ireland, Britain and Spain —

are especially vulnerable, as are several Eastern European countries and other emerging markets, which are running steep current account deficits and low foreign currency reserves.

Ireland's finance minister, Brian Lenihan, traced his country's predicament back to Lehman Brothers, saying that the American authorities "were mistaken in permitting that bank to go to the wall because it has had very serious consequences for the world financial system."

The Irish plan guarantees bank deposits and debt for customers and creditors of six banks. That makes the government responsible for $400 billion, twice the country's economic output.

Experts predict a rash of bank failures in Europe, though some say the process may prove less politically fraught than in the United States, given the tradition of nationalization there.

So far, the hurdle to a broader plan has been the European Union's legal and political restrictions that require burden-sharing and consensus. "The Europeans are more rigid and rule-based than the Americans," said Simon Johnson, a former chief economist at the International Monetary Fund. "But when things get bad enough, they'll find the flexibility."

One red flag, he said, is UBS, the giant Swiss bank that is heavily exposed to mortgage-related securities and is headquartered in a small country that is not a member of the union. "Opinion is divided as to whether Switzerland could bail out UBS," Mr. Johnson said.

Beyond individual banks, the United States has to worry about the health of major holders of American government debt, from Russia and China to oil-producing states in the Middle East.

Russia is a particular concern, experts said. With oil prices swooning and its own banks in crisis, it is coming under financial strain. If the Russians were to sell off their American debt holdings, it could depress the dollar and multiply the cost of a bailout.

Russia has already begun whittling its vast foreign reserves to finance an aid program for its banks. American officials said shifts in foreign holdings of American debt were not great.

Other big creditors, like China, are in better shape financially, according to experts. But even there, growth is slowing, as trans-Pacific trade dries up. Should that contraction be traumatic and cause a banking crisis, it could lead the Chinese to sell their American holdings, these experts say.

The dollar has also remained remarkably stable, given the turmoil on Wall Street and in Washington — another sign, economists said, that foreign investors have not yet lost faith in the United States. Partly, though, that reflects a paucity of other safe places to invest money.

"We would run into a huge problem if foreigners lost confidence," said Kenneth S. Rogoff, an economist at Harvard. "The rest of the world will give us several swings at the ball before they give up on us."

(Carter Dougherty contributed reporting from Frankfurt and Andrew Kramer from Moscow.)

第 2 章

UNIT 2

INTERNATIONAL FINANCE

• Text •

背景参考

次贷危机的源头是次级抵押贷款，即一些贷款机构，向信用程度较差和收入不高的借款人提供的贷款。近年美国等国家放松购房信贷标准(不用付首期，不用收入证明，也不计较抵押单位的质素等)，形成次级房贷市场。次级房屋信贷经过贷款机构及华尔街用财务工程方法加以估算、组合、包装，就以票据或证券产品形式，在抵押二级市场上出卖，用高息吸引其他金融机构和对冲基金购买。2006 年美国房地产市场恶化以及美元利率多次加息，令次级房屋信贷的拖欠以及坏账增加，次级房屋信贷产品的价格大跌，直接导致欧美以及澳洲不少金融机构都出现财政危机，甚至面临破产，牵动全球信贷出现收缩。

投资银行是最典型的投资性金融机构，一般认为，投资银行是在资本市场上为企业发行债券、股票，筹集长期资金提供中介服务的金融机构，主要从事证券承销、公司购并与资产重组、公司理财、基金管理等业务。2008 年在美国次贷危机的影响下，世界很多投资金融机构陆续破产。

Lehman Brothers(美国雷曼兄弟公司) 创建于 1850 年，主要为全球公司、机构、政府和投资者的金融需求提供服务，曾经是美国第四大投资银行。受次级房贷风暴连锁效应波及，2008 年 9 月 15 日雷曼兄弟公司宣布申请破产保护，负债达

6,130 亿美元。

Equity Office Properties Trust(办公物业信托公司) 是美国最大的办公房产投资商,由 Samuel Zell 创建于 1976 年。2007 年 2 月被 Blackstone(百仕通集团) 收购,此次收购是数额最大的一笔私营股权收购案。

Dutch bank ABN Amro(荷兰银行),历史可以追溯到 1824 年,通过不断合并,1990 年成立荷兰银行,是一家全球领先的跨国银行。2007 年 10 月被 Fortis Bank(比利时富通银行)、Royal Bank of Scotland Group(苏格兰皇家银行) 和 Santander of Spain(西班牙国际银行) 所组成的银行财团全面收购。

Merrill Lynch(美林公司) 创办于 1914 年 1 月 7 日,业务有个人理财计划,经纪证券买卖,公司顾问,外汇与商品交易,衍生工具与研究等。2008 年 9 月 14 日以大约 440 亿美元的价格出售给 Bank of America Corp(美国银行)。

Wachovia(美联银行) 于 2001 年由美联银行同瓦霍维亚银行合并而成,是美国最大的多样化金融服务公司之一,向客户提供银行业务、资产管理、财富管理、企业及投资银行业务产品及服务等。2008 年 10 月被 Wells Fargo & Co. (富国银行) 以 145 亿美元的价格收购。

Washington Mutual(华盛顿互惠银行) 简称 WAMU(华互银行),建立于 1889 年,是全美第四大居民住房抵押服务供应商,也是一家区域性的金融服务公司,为消费者和中小业户提供多样化的产品和服务。2008 年 9 月 25 日由摩根大通以 19 亿美元的超低价收购。

Deals That Were Doomed from the Start: A Look Back

By ROB COX

Published: *October* 6, 2008, 11:54 *pm*

Business Column of The New York Times

Edited by Andrew Ross Sorkin

In hindsight, we all have perfect vision. **But there are some merger and acquisition[1] transactions concocted at the height of the credit bubble — and even after it burst — that looked ill-fated from the get-go[2].** With few exceptions they proved deadly for the executives who engineered them and shareholders who supported them.

The following deals are emblematic of an era fueled by cheap credit[3] and corporate animal spirits gone wild. This list is by no means comprehensive — **the process of stripping leverage from the global financial landscape will almost certainly provide more fodder.**

A BRIDGE TO BANKRUPTCY Lehman Brothers' deep involvement (alongside Tishman Speyer Properties) in buying Archstone-Smith Trust[4] for $22.2 billion was not the reason the investment bank filed for bankruptcy in September, ending the longtime run of Richard S. Fuld Jr., its chief executive. **But the May 2007 deal was representative of the concentrated risks Lehman had taken in the property market.** These in turn sparked questions from investors about the way Lehman valued many of its assets and whether the firm had sufficient capital against potential write-downs[5].

Here's how the deal got into trouble. Right after Blackstone[6]'s successful swoop on Sam Zell's Equity Office Properties Trust — and quick piecemeal sale of many of its assets at a profit — Lehman kicked off its own version of the deal. With its partner Tishman Speyer[7], Lehman took Archstone's portfolio of residential properties[8] private, injecting equity and cobbling together a $4.6 billion package of so-called "bridge equity." **The Lehman-led group put up equity, instead of an old-fashioned bridge loan[9], placing the group at the bottom of the capital structure and in a highly vulnerable position in the event of an Archstone bankruptcy.**

The idea was to hand off the risk to investors later, which happened in the Equity Office Properties deal. But Lehman couldn't pull it off and, with billions of dollars of debt linked to the deal that had also fallen in value, wound up with $2.4 billion of Archstone equity on its balance sheet[10].

PYRRHIC VICTORY Barclays kicked off a banking scrum of epic proportions in March 2007 when it began talks to acquire the Dutch bank ABN Amro. Thankfully for Barclays[11] shareholders, the British bank was outbid by a consortium that included Fortis of Belgium[12] (led at the time by Jean-Paul Votron), the Royal Bank of Scotland Group[13] and Santander of Spain[14], which paid $98 billion in total, largely in cash, for ABN.

When the credit crunch hit, it became clear how badly timed their purchase was. The governments of Belgium and the Netherlands dismembered Fortis, the weakest of the trio, with its Belgian arm being sold to France's BNP Paribas[15] and its Dutch arm nationalized. The Royal Bank fared better — it was able to replenish its coffers with a $24.4 billion rights issue earlier this year. Even so, its shares have been battered and the market's view of its creditworthiness has suffered. Santander escaped relatively unblemished. It flipped ABN's Italian assets for a 3.2 billion euro profit only a month after buying them.

SUBPRIME BINGE Just as the housing market was hitting the skids, Merrill Lynch handed over $1.3 billion in September 2006 for First Franklin Financial, a business that lent money to homebuyers that other banks wouldn't touch. First Franklin was not the straw that broke Merrill Lynch's back. Nor was Merrill the only Wall Street firm picking up mortgage originators.

But Merrill's purchase of First Franklin was the largest of the crop and the price it paid stood out given mounting evidence of a housing slowdown. Merrill, led at the time by E. Stanley O'Neal, made clear its strategy was not to hold these mortgages from sketchy borrowers for long, but to repackage them and sell the risk on to someone else.

Within a year it became obvious this was not happening anymore. Merrill was left holding billions of such dross on its books, though most of it originated before its First Franklin deal. The end result: O'Neal was fired, Merrill took more than $30 billion of write-downs and was forced to raise capital on dilutive terms, and Merrill last month sold itself in a hurry to Bank of America.

DODGY MORTGAGES California dreaming did not get G. Kennedy Thompson, the Wachovia chairman, very far. In May 2006 he engineered the $26 billion purchase of Golden West Financial. The deal looked fraught with risk. Wachovia had paid three times Golden West's book value just as the California housing market was starting to turn.

Moreover, most of Golden West's mortgage book was composed of riskier option adjustable rate mortgages[16]. Two years on, Wachovia ousted Mr. Thompson after taking stinging write-downs on many of these assets.

Wachovia's future is still up in the air.

SOUR DEAL TPG's failed attempt to recapitalize Washington Mutual in April is unlikely to bring down the private equity group in the way other deals wounded Lehman, Merrill, Wachovia and Fortis. But it serves as a painful lesson for an industry struggling to prove its worth at a time when credit is scarce.

David Bonderman, who heads TPG[17], led a $7 billion capital-raising for the bank that saw him and his investors sink $2 billion into WaMu. While risky, it looked as if TPG was receiving protection against further deterioration at WaMu. **The bouquet included WaMu stock at a discount, in-the-money convertible securities and warrants, lots of fees and an anti-dilution "ratchet" that made it punitive for WaMu to raise additional capital.** Two weeks ago, regulators declared WaMu insolvent and sold its carcass to JPMorgan[18] for $1.9 billion. TPG's investment was wiped out.

难点注释

1 merger and acquisition 收购与合并

商务中，收购是两家公司联合成一家公司。这种行为通常是自愿的，并通过购入资产或股票以获得对卖方企业的控制权。合并也是一种收购，是一家公司对另一家公司的购买，合并既可以是友好的也可以是敌意的。

In business or economics a merger is a combination of two companies into one larger company. Such actions are commonly voluntary and involve stock swap or cash payment to the target. An acquisition, also known as a takeover or a buyout, is the buying of one company (the 'target') by another. An acquisition may be friendly or hostile. (*From Wikipedia, the free encyclopedia*)

2 ill-fated from the get-go 从一开始就注定的厄运

3 cheap credit: the credit with lower interest 低息信贷

4 Archstone-Smith Trust 公寓住宅投资信托公司

2001 年以并购方式成立的 AST 公司是美国第三大房地产投资信托公司。其核心业务是经营管理其在美国各主要城市的住宅公寓。2007 年 5 月由私营建筑商以 155 万美元并购。

Archstone-Smith Trust, formed from a 2001 merger, is the third largest

United States Real Estate Investment Trust (REIT). Its core business is the ownership and management of residential apartment buildings in major metropolitan areas across the United States. Since May 2007 it has been in the process of a US$15.5 billion takeover by a private real estate builder-operator firm in alliance with several major United States investment banks. (*From Wikipedia, the free encyclopedia*)

5 write-downs 账面资产减值

Reducing the book value of an asset because it is overvalued compared to the market value.

6 Blackstone 百仕通集团

全世界最大的独立另类资产管理机构之一，美国规模最大的上市投资管理公司，其另类资产管理业务包括企业私募股权基金、房地产基金、对冲基金、夹层基金、高级债券基金、私人对冲基金和封闭式基金等。

Blackstone is a leading global alternative asset manager and provider of financial advisory services listed on the New York Stock Exchange. Its alternative asset management businesses include the management of Corporate Private Equity funds, Real Estate funds and Marketable Alternative Asset Management funds etc.

7 Tishman Speyer 铁狮门房地产公司

美国铁狮门房地产公司成立于1978年，是全球一流的房地产投资与开发公司，在全球18个城市开发或管理着包括洛克菲勒中心在内的41宗商业与居住房地产项目；并已经成功开发并获取了资产价值超过150亿美元、面积超过520万平方米的土地投资组合，是擅长开发与管理密切结合的房地产企业。

Tishman Speyer is one of the leading owners, developers, operators, and managers of first-class real estate in the world, having managed a portfolio of assets since its inception of over 115 million square feet and more than 92,000 residential units in major metropolitan areas across the United States, Europe, Latin America and Asia. (from www.tishmanspeyer.com)

8 residential properties 房地产

9 bridge loan 过桥贷款

在国外通常是指中介机构在安排较为复杂的中长期贷款前，为满足其服务公司正常运营的资金需要而提供的短期融资。

A short-term loan that is used until a person or company secures permanent financing or removes an existing obligation. This type of financing allows the user to meet current obligations by providing immediate cash flow. The loans are short-term (up to one year) with relatively high interest rates and are backed by some form of collateral such as real estate or inventory. (*From Wikipedia, the free encyclopedia*)

10 balance sheet 资产负债表

资产负债表反映了企业在一定日期的财务状况，即资产、负债和业主权益状况的会计报表。

In financial accounting, a balance sheet or statement of financial position is a summary of a person's or organization's balances. Assets, liabilities and ownership equity are listed as of a specific date, such as the end of its financial year. (*From Wikipedia, the free encyclopedia*)

11 Barclays 巴克莱银行

英国最大的商业银行之一，1862年成立，是位于汇丰银行和苏格兰皇家银行之后的英国第三大银行公司，经营信用卡、抵押贷款、代管及租赁业务，此外还提供私人银行业务。

Barclays is a major global financial services provider engaged in retail and commercial banking, credit cards, investment banking, wealth management and investment management services, with an extensive international presence in Europe, the Americas, Africa and Asia. (*From www.barclays.com*)

12 Fortis of Belgium 比利时富通银行

富通集团旗下企业，成立于2000年3月21日，总部设在比利时布鲁塞尔。是由比利时通用银行(General Bank)、荷兰 Meespierson 银行、比利时 Aslk/Cger Bank 储蓄银行与荷兰 Vsb Bank 储蓄银行合并组成的欧洲第十大银行。涉足商业银行业务、网上银行业务和个人银行及资产管理业务。

It is a company that was active in banking, insurance, and investment management. In 2007 it was the 20th largest business in the world by revenue, but most of the company was sold in parts in 2008, with only insurance activities remaining. (*From Wikipedia, the free encyclopedia*)

13 the Royal Bank of Scotland Group 苏格兰皇家银行集团

建于1727年，总部设在英国的爱丁堡，是欧洲领先的金融服务集团，也是英国最大的银行，其业务遍及英国和世界各地。该银行在英国的法人、个人及海外银行业中排名第一，在零售银行业及私人汽车保险业中排名第二。

It is one of the retail banking subsidiaries of the Royal Bank of Scotland Group plc, and together with NatWest and Ulster Bank, provides branch banking facilities in the United Kingdom. (From Wikipedia, the free encyclopedia)

14 Santander of Spain 西班牙国际银行有限公司

西班牙国际银行有限公司也叫桑坦德银行，是全球知名的多功能银行，该银行目前在全世界排名第九，在欧元区排名第二。其北京代表处成立于1993年。在符合中国金融法规的前提下，西班牙国际银行有限公司通过代表处的平台为中国的基础设施建设提供出口信贷、贸易融资等。

It traces its ancestry to the 1857 provincial bank of Santander (in northern Spain), and has grown subsequently by mergers and takeovers. It is the largest bank in the euro area, which originated in Santander, Cantabria, Spain. More information refers to Wikipedia.

15 France's BNP Paribas 法国巴黎银行

2000年5月，法国两家主要商业银行巴黎国民银行与巴黎巴银行正式合并为法国巴黎银行。通过不断开发扩展商业及金融业务品种，法国巴黎银行已经成为一间真正的国际银行，并且在公司银行、资本市场、国际私人银行及资产管理等业务方面成绩卓越。

It was created on 23 May 2000 through the merger of Banque Nationale de Paris (BNP) and Paribas. Together with Société Générale and Crédit Lyonnais (now known as LCL), it is one of the "three old" banks of France. And it is one of the main banks in Europe.

16 option adjustable rate mortgages 自由的可调整利率贷款

17 TPG: abbr. of Texas Pacific Group 得克萨斯太平洋集团

美国最大的私人股权投资公司之一。1992年创立，业务主要是为公司转型、管理层收购和资本重组提供资金支持，尤其在通过杠杆收购、资本结构调整、分拆、合资以及重组而进行的全球股市和私募投资上有着丰富经验。

TPG Capital (formerly Texas Pacific Group) is one of the largest private equity investment firms globally, focused on leveraged buyout, growth capital and leveraged re-capitalization investments in distressed companies and turnaround situations. (*From Wikipedia, the free encyclopedia*)

18 JPMorgan Chase&Co. 摩根大通银行

由大通银行，J. P. 摩根公司及富林明集团在 2000 年完成合并。合并后的新公司在银团贷款、金融衍生产品和外汇交易业务上位居全球前列。而摩根则将更加专注于资产管理业务。

JPMorgan is one of the oldest financial services firms in the world. Formed in 2000 when Chase Manhattan Corporation acquired J. P. Morgan & Co., the firm serves millions of consumers in the United States and many of the world's most prominent corporate, institutional and governmental clients. (*From Wikipedia, the free encyclopedia*)

精华长句

1 But there are some merger and acquisition transactions concocted at the height of the credit bubble — and even after it burst — that looked ill-fated from the get-go.

但是在信贷泡沫高峰时期，甚至是其破裂后所出现的一些收购与合并交易，从一开始就注定了它们的厄运。

2 the process of stripping leverage from the global financial landscape will almost certainly provide more fodder.

从全球金融格局看，杠杆拆离过程几乎能提供更多的思考。

3 But the May 2007 deal was representative of the concentrated risks Lehman had taken in the property market.

但是 2007 年 5 月集中体现雷曼的风险的交易在房地产市场产生了。

4 The Lehman-led group put up equity, instead of an old-fashioned bridge loan, placing the group at the bottom of the capital structure and in a highly vulnerable position in the event of an Archstone bankruptcy.

雷曼公司为首的集团所提出替代旧式过桥贷款的产权，在 Archstone 公司破产事件中，使得集团处于资本机构的底层并且处于高度易损的位置。

5 When the credit crunch hit, it became clear how badly timed their purchase was.

当出现信贷紧缩时，他们的收购多么的糟糕就会非常明显。

6 But Merrill's purchase of First Franklin was the largest of the crop and the price it paid stood out given mounting evidence of a housing slowdown.

但是，美林收购第一富兰克林却是最大的收获，在房市下滑的大量证据前，它支付的价格是非常突出的。

7 The bouquet included WaMu stock at a discount, in-the-money convertible securities and warrants, lots of fees and an anti-dilution "ratchet" that made it punitive for WaMu to raise additional capital.

保护资金包括华盛顿互惠银行折扣股票、溢价可转换债券和认股权证，大量的费用，以及反稀释"棘轮"，即华盛顿互惠银行用于对额外增资的惩罚。

理解练习题

1 How did Lehman Brothers get into trouble in buying Archstone-Smith Trust？

2 How much did ABN Amro get in acquiring? Who paid in cash?

3 What business did First Franklin Financial do before 2006?

4 Who and how much bought WaMu's carcass?

讨论

1 Discussion：bridge equity. What's your idea of "a bridge to bankruptcy"？

2 What do you think of "subprime binge"？

3 What's your opinion of "credit bubble" and "subprime crisis"？

• Extensive Reading •

Mailing Our Way to Solvency

By MICHAEL LIND

Published：*October* 5，2008

Opinion Column of The New York Times

Washington

AMERICA'S financial landscape is changing before our eyes. The absorption of major Wall Street investment banks by commercial banks threatens to create colossal universal banks that are too big to fail and might need to be bailed out in the future. Meanwhile, the structure of public and private finance in the United States chronically fails to address four problems: the almost 10 percent of Americans without a bank account; the concerns of all Americans about the security of their savings; the growing indebtedness of the country to foreign governments and financial institutions; and underinvestment in public assets like sewer systems and bridges.

These four problems may seem unrelated. But they can be addressed in the United States, as they have been in similar countries, by a single institution that is at once new and old: the postal savings bank.

Britain created the first postal savings bank in 1861, and by the early 20th century many other nations had postal savings bank systems. The details vary among countries, but the idea is simple: use the one government institution that can be found in most neighborhoods and rural areas — the post office — to encourage small savings and a habit of thrift.

Well, we don't do things that way in America, you might object. On the contrary — we did! In 1910, Congress created a postal savings system. The Post Office offered small savings accounts to individual Americans. The system boomed during the Depression and World War II, with a balance of more than $3 billion in 1947 — almost $30 billion in today's dollars.

But F. D. I. C. insurance of private bank accounts removed the advantage of security from the postal savings system, and its fixed 2 percent interest rate was uncompetitive. By 1966, deposits had fallen to $344 million (still more than $2 billion when adjusted for inflation) and Congress voted to abolish the system.

A new postal savings system should be part of America's post-meltdown financial architecture. When Congress created the postal savings system nearly a century ago, one of its goals was to encourage savings among the large number of low-income immigrants. A new system would help today's immigrants as well as the native poor. Banks are not interested in people with so little money, many of whom are preyed upon by payday lenders and credit card companies.

A postal bank could also supply middle-class and affluent Americans with an extra layer of financial security. The accounts would be limited to a small amount per person. They would provide a government-guaranteed, low-risk, low-return investment, even for those who put most of their financial assets in conventional bank accounts and the stock market.

Non-Western countries like Japan and India have used postal savings systems to reduce their economic dependence on foreign investors. What better way to reduce the dependence of the United States on Asian banks and petrostate sovereign wealth funds than a system that pools the modest savings of ordinary Americans to pay down the national debt?

A revived postal savings bank, in addition to holding much of the national debt, could provide a purely domestic source of savings that could be tapped by a national infrastructure bank. There is growing support for such a government-chartered institution, which could borrow money to modernize roads, power grids and sewage systems; according to one estimate, we need \$1.6 trillion over five years. That money is unlikely to come from Congress.

Japan's postal savings bank, privatized during the heyday of market fundamentalism a few years ago, was criticized because it encouraged too much saving and too much investment in infrastructure. If only the United States had such problems!

When the financial crisis has passed, Americans will need to rebuild our financial system. A new postal savings system should be part of the plan.

(*Michael Lind is a fellow at the New America Foundation, where he directs the American Infrastructure Initiative.*)

第 3 章

UNIT 3

INVESTMENT

• Text •

背景参考

为应对次贷危机，美国联邦储备委员会于 2008 年 7 月 14 日通过一系列规范住房抵押贷款活动的新措施，以保护低收入购房者免遭各种贷款陷阱。

美联储打击不良借贷的新举措包括：禁止放贷者向没有收入证明的借款人提供贷款；放贷方必须确保风险借款人有余款用于支付税收和保险；限制放贷方惩罚提前还款的风险借款人。由于一般次贷项目具有越往后还款利率越高的特点，放贷方不希望借方提前还款；如果借方除住房本身抵押的价值外没有其他支付房贷的能力，放贷方不得提供贷款等等。

新举措规定对于贷方的违规行为，无需借方本人举证。这是在消费者保护组织的呼吁下，美联储专门做出的修正，以便借方对违规行为提出投诉。

新举措对欺骗行为进行严格监管。由于拖欠抵押贷款和丧失抵押品赎回权的案例数量快速增长，给借款方、所在社区以及国家经济带来巨大代价。由于"次贷"借入者多为低收入阶层或信用记录不佳者，这些人无力继续还贷，造成美国房贷市场抵押赎回权丧失案例剧增。新举措规定，今后所有抵押贷款项目需明示利率、月供等相关信息。美联储还将监管和打击带有欺骗或误导性质的放贷广告。在规范抵押贷款市场的其他活动方面，美联储禁止交易商胁迫或怂恿房屋评估师歪曲真实房价；放贷方收到月供当天就需给借方账户记上信用记录。

对于美联储的新规定，各方持不同的看法。一些消费者保护组织抱怨，美联储的新规定仍然缺乏力度；放贷方担心，这些措施过于强硬，限制了消费者的抵押贷款选择。还有人认为，这些新规定的有效性近期恐怕无从验证，因为在当前的住房和信贷市场上，购房者数量大幅减少，而美联储刻意打击的不良放贷行为也随市场低迷而无法继续存在。尽管这些举措属于亡羊补牢，但对美国政府应对次贷危机、缓解经济低迷、恢复市场活力、恢复投资者信心的确非常重要。

2008 年 10 月 3 日，布什签署了 7000 亿美元的救市计划。

2008 年 10 月 8 日，各大央行同时行动对金融市场的动荡作出明确的回应，接连宣布降息；美联储宣布降息 50 个基点至 1.50%，欧洲央行、英国央行、加拿大央行、瑞典央行和瑞士央行也纷纷降息 50 个基点；澳大利亚联邦储备银行将银行基准利率下调 1% 至 6.00%；以色列央行也宣布降息 50 个基点至 3.75%。

2009 年 10 月 9 日，韩国、日本、中国香港地区、中国台湾地区和印度尼西亚等有关当局，纷纷采取措施放松了货币政策，向银行注资。

New Regulations Sure to Accompany Bailout

Lawmakers are expected to focus first on mortgage standards, regulatory enforcement and establishing rules for markets. [1]

By Michael A. Hiltzik

September 25, 2008

Business Column of Los Angeles Times

Once the smoke clears from the conflagration in the financial markets, Congress and the next administration will face a new challenge: how to keep the next fire from burning down the house.

New regulations, or better enforcement of the old, are certain to be high on the agenda.

"We've got to have the most dramatic rethinking of our regulatory structure since the New Deal," says former Securities and Exchange Commissioner Harvey J. Goldschmid, now a law professor at Columbia University.

Legal and political observers believe lawmakers will probably focus first on three broad areas: tightening regulation of mortgage lending, streamlining regulatory enforcement and establishing oversight of unregulated financial markets.[2]

Mortgage lending is an obvious target because so much of the bad debt dragging down banks originated with the lax practices of brokers and lenders, who handed out loans to poorly qualified buyers with scant collateral.

"The 'three Cs' of mortgage lending have always been credit, collateral, capacity to pay," says Edward Kramer, executive vice president for regulatory services at consulting firm Wolters Kluver Financial Services. "These are the most basic elements of loan underwriting, and we lost sight of that."

Lawmakers may also try to revamp[3] the patchwork of government authority over banks. Banks are now regulated by four agencies — the Comptroller of the Currency, the Federal Deposit Insurance Corp., the Office of Thrift Supervision and the Federal Reserve — with overlapping jurisdictions.

Treasury Secretary Henry M. Paulson proposed such an overhaul in March. His plan involved converting the FED[4] into a banking "supercop" and merging the SEC[5] and the Commodity Futures Trading Commission[6] into a single regulator.

At the time, many observers saw his proposal as a pretext for deregulation[7]. But in a deeper financial crisis, the idea is gaining new currency.

"This is clearly a system that was built a piece at a time as opposed to on a blank sheet of paper," says Donald P. Gould, president of Gould Asset Management, a Claremont investment firm. "That has led to a lot of finger-pointing and made it easy for things to fall into the gaps."[8]

Lawmakers may also try to bring unregulated markets, such as those for arcane derivative securities[9] known as credit default swaps, under control.

The case against regulation has been that these markets are dominated by sophisticated investors such as hedge funds and other major institutions that don't need government oversight to protect them. But the market for credit default swaps alone has grown to $44 trillion in face value — so gigantic that a glitch at any large participant poses the risk of global destabilization.

Credit default swaps are complex securities that allow investors to speculate on the chances that a banking firm will default on its obligations. Like several of the initiatives likely to surface in the wake of the crisis, efforts to regulate these swaps are not new.

In 1998, the Commodity Futures Trading Commission proposed bringing credit default swaps and other risky derivatives — by then a $100-trillion business — under its jurisdiction. The move followed the collapse of Long Term Capital Management, a hedge fund[10] that owned $1.25 trillion in derivatives contracts, supported by a bare $4 billion in capital.

The proposal led to a ferocious attack on then-CFTC Chairwoman Brooksley Born by her fellow government regulators, and the plan was never approved. Two years later, Congress exempted over-the-counter derivatives from any CFTC regulation. The exemption was heavily lobbied for by Enron Corp., then riding high as a derivatives merchant, and sponsored by then-Sen. Phil Gramm Co.

But thanks to the pressure of impending disaster, the landscape has shifted on the issue. Just this week, SEC Chairman Christopher Cox begged Congress for jurisdiction[11] over the same derivatives, urging lawmakers to give him authority "to enhance investor protection and ensure the operation of fair and orderly markets."

Experts say that among the most urgent fixes for today's regulatory system is to reverse the decline of disclosure — the bedrock principle of financial regulation.

"I'm a big believer that you can get away with less regulation if the market can get the information it needs," says Lynn E. Turner, a former SEC chief accountant. "When people can make so much money behind closed doors and can't be caught, they do very bad things."

Over the last decade, however, regulators have consistently allowed less disclosure. In 2001, a blue-ribbon committee of bankers advocated a dramatic expansion of banks' disclosures of the risks of their credit portfolio[12]. The recommendations were rejected by the Federal Reserve Board.

The dearth of disclosure not only kept corporate managements in the dark about the risks in their portfolios, but also prevented government overseers from detecting the coming catastrophe.

"We need to set up a framework that will give government the ability to know in systemic terms when something is going wrong," Goldschmid says.

The dimensions of the regulatory failure in the current crisis may provide support to relieve another long-standing problem with America's oversight agencies — their relative poverty.

The SEC's 2007 budget, for example, was $882 million. That was only slightly higher than the $812-million budget of the Financial Industry Regulatory Authority, the self-regulatory agency for the country's securities brokerage firms. **The SEC's jurisdiction includes not only brokers but also supervision of stock exchanges and exchange-listed companies and the ferreting out of fraud.**

The burden on the SEC and other regulators is only going to become more onerous[13]. This week the Federal Reserve acquired jurisdiction over the giant investment banks Goldman Sachs and Morgan Stanley, which received approval to remake themselves as bank holding companies, bringing them for the first time under the eyes of Fed banking examiners.

"Unfortunately, the current examiner force is not yet prepared for this increased oversight responsibility," says Mark T. Williams, a former examiner at the Federal Reserve banks of San Francisco and Boston who is now on the faculty of the Boston University School of Management.

"We need sophisticated, experienced staff, and that staff has to be paid better than it's paid today so people with home mortgages and kids in college can't be enticed away," adds Ernest T. Patrikis, a former general counsel at the New York Federal Reserve Bank and former executive at American International Group.

Several experts caution that one looming danger is overreaction — too much regulation harbors its own risks. One example may be the SEC's initiative last week in barring short selling in hundreds of financial stocks. (Short sellers borrow shares of companies they expect to lose value, then sell them in hopes of making a profit by buying the shares back at reduced prices.)

The SEC's step was aimed at stemming a downdraft in shares of banks and investment companies. Even with the ban, many of the protected stocks have fallen sharply in price. Many market professionals believe short sellers play an indispensable role in identifying overvalued companies.

"If you take short sellers out of the market, you've got the government setting prices," Turner says. He advocates less draconian measures, including enforcing rules requiring short sellers to actually borrow the shares they are shorting rather than merely promising to locate them if necessary.

难点注释

1 Lawmakers are expected to focus first on mortgage standards, regulatory enforcement and establishing rules for markets.

立法者预计将重点首先集中于抵押贷款的标准、监管执法和建立市场规则方面。

2 Legal and political observers believe lawmakers will probably focus first on three broad areas: tightening regulation of mortgage lending, streamlining regulatory enforcement and establishing oversight of unregulated financial markets.

法律和政治观察家认为,立法者将重点首先集中于三大领域:按揭贷款的调控,简化监管执法,建立对未受制约的金融市场的监管。

3 revamp 修补

to patch up or renovate, repair or restore

4 FED: The Board of Governors of The Federal Reserve System 美国联邦储备系统管理委员会

是联邦储备系统(Federal Reserve System)的核心机构,简称美联储。它是一个联邦政府机构,其办公地点位于美国华盛顿特区。基本职能是通过三种主要的手段(公开市场操作、规定银行准备金比率、批准各联邦储备银行要求的贴现率)来实现相关货币政策。

FED provides a detailed look at the structure, responsibilities, and operations of the Federal Reserve System. Revised in 2005 to reflect changes in monetary, regulatory, and other policy areas. (*www.federalreserve.gov*)

5 SEC: Securities and Exchange Commission 证券交易委员会

于1934年根据《1934年证券交易法》而成立,是直属美国联邦的独立准司法机构,负责美国的证券监督和管理工作,是美国证券行业的最高机构。旨在监督证券法规的实施。

The U.S. Securities and Exchange Commission (commonly known as the SEC) is an independent agency of the United States government, which holds primary responsibility for enforcing the federal securities laws and regulating the securities industry, the nation's stock and options exchanges, and other electronic securities markets. (*From Wikipedia*, *the free encyclopedia*)

6 Commodity Futures Trading Commission(CFTC) 商品期货交易委员会

根据美国1974年商品期货交易委员会法成立的美国联邦机构，旨在确保期货市场的公开及高效运作。委员会共有五名由总统委任的期货市场委员，并须获得参议院的批准。

Congress created the Commodity Futures Trading Commission (CFTC) in 1974 as an independent agency with the mandate to regulate commodity futures and option markets in the United States. (*from www.cftc.gov*)

7 deregulation 放松管制、违反规定

the act of freeing from regulation, especially from governmental regulations

8 "That has led to a lot of finger-pointing and made it easy for things to fall into the gaps."

"这导致了很多指责，并且很容易使事情无果而终。"

9 derivative securities 衍生证券

也称衍生工具，是一种证券，其价值依赖于其他更基本的标的变量。目前包括远期合约、期货、期权、互换等。

Derivative securities usually takes the form of an agreement to buy or sell an asset or item (commodity, property, security) at a fixed price on or before a certain date. Derivative securities are traded on exchanges like other financial instruments, and their value varies with the value of the underlying assets (which are traded separately from the derivatives). Futures contracts, forward contracts, options and swaps are some common types of derivatives used in hedging or to gain leverage. (*http://www.businessdictionary.com/definition/derivative-security.html*)

10 a hedge fund 对冲基金

投资基金的一种形式。这种基金采用各种交易手段，如卖空、杠杆操作、程序交易、互换交易、套利交易、衍生品种等进行对冲、换位、套头、套期来赚取巨额利润。这些概念已经超出了传统的防止风险、保障收益的操作范畴。加之发起和设立对冲基金的法律门槛远低于互惠基金，使之风险进一步加大。为了保护投资者，北美的证券管理机构将其列入高风险投资品种行列，严格限制普通投资者介入。

A hedge fund is an investment fund open to a limited range of investors that is permitted by regulators to undertake a wider range of investment and trading activities than other investment funds, and that, in general, pays a performance fee to its investment manager. Every hedge fund has its own investment strategy that determines the type of investments and the methods of investment it undertakes. Hedge funds, as a class, invest in a broad range of investments including shares, debt and commodities. (*http://en.wikipedia.org/wiki/Hedge_fund*)

11 jurisdiction 管辖、管辖权

the right and power to interpret and apply the law

12 disclosures of the risks of their credit portfolio 信贷组合的风险披露

13 onerous 繁重的

not easily borne, wearing

精华长句

1 Once the smoke clears from the conflagration in the financial markets, Congress and the next administration will face a new challenge: how to keep the next fire from burning down the house.

一旦硝烟从金融市场的战火中散尽，国会和下届政府将面临一个新的挑战，即如何保护家园免遭后续危机的影响。

2 The proposal led to a ferocious attack on then-CFTC Chairwoman Brooksley Born by her fellow government regulators, and the plan was never approved. Two years later, Congress exempted over-the-counter derivatives from any CFTC regulation. The exemption was heavily lobbied for by Enron Corp., then riding high as a derivatives merchant, and sponsored by then-Sen. Phil Gramm. Co.

该提议导致了对以合作政府监管而闻名的商品期货交易委员会主席 Brooksley 的猛烈攻击，该计划从未获得批准。两年以后，美国国会将场外衍生工具从商品期货交易委员的管辖中豁免。该豁免源于安然公司（当时风头正猛的衍生品厂商）的大量游说，并由当时的 Sen. Phil Gramm 公司提供赞助。

3 The dearth of disclosure not only kept corporate managements in the dark

about the risks in their portfolios, but also prevented government overseers from detecting the coming catastrophe.

信息披露的缺乏不仅会使公司对风险的管理不明确，同时也会使政府监管人员难以发现未来的灾难。

4 The SEC's jurisdiction includes not only brokers but also supervision of stock exchanges and exchange-listed companies and the ferreting out of fraud.

美国证券交易委员会的管辖范围不仅包括经纪人，而且包括证券公司和上市公司以及欺诈行为。

5 Several experts caution that one looming danger is overreaction — too much regulation harbors its own risks. One example may be the SEC's initiative last week in barring short selling in hundreds of financial stocks. (Short sellers borrow shares of companies they expect to lose value, then sell them in hopes of making a profit by buying the shares back at reduced prices.)

一些专家警告说，一个迫在眉睫的危险是过度反应，过多的管理条例本身即隐匿着大量的风险。

讨论

1 What is the International Investment?

2 What is the favorable investment environment?

3 What are the advantages that International Investment bring about to a country?

• Extensive Reading •

Global Stocks: Should You Pull Out?

by Ben Steverman

October 7, 2008, 12:01 *AM*

Investing Column of Business Week

This crisis started in the U. S. , but investors have seen huge losses overseas. It does not seem fair. The current financial crisis started in the U. S. , but stock markets in the rest of the world have felt more pain.

That's not to say that American investors haven't felt the effects of the global sell-off, which accelerated on Oct. 6. U. S. investors have spent years shifting money into booming overseas markets, but now that strategy is backfiring as overseas stocks tumble.

The MSCI EAFE Index (EFA)—an abbreviation for Morgan Stanley Capital International Europe, Australasia & Far East—is off 36% this year, while the Standard & Poor's 500, the broad U. S. index, is down 28% by comparison. Stocks in emerging markets such as China, India, and Russia have performed even worse, with one measure, the Vanguard Emerging Markets index (VWO), off 45%.

Adding to American investors' global investing woes is a rising dollar. If U. S. investors buy equities priced in a foreign currency such as the euro, they benefit when the dollar weakens—which it has for the past few years — but are hurt when the dollar gains ground. The euro has fallen almost 16% from its peak of $1.60 this summer.

No Coordinated Effort

Overseas losses deepened on Oct. 6 on new evidence that the financial crisis is spreading worldwide, especially to banks in Europe.

While the U. S. has approved a $700 billion bailout plan for its financial industry, "It's pretty evident Europe has to make a coordinated effort to do something about the financial markets" as well, says Madelynn Matlock, portfolio manager of the Huntington International Equity Fund (HIEAX).

Economists have been worrying about a U. S. slowdown for the past year, but many professional investors now also expect a global slowdown. That's showing up in the stock markets' relative performance. "One can make the case that the U. S. is further along in this economic slowdown," says Wasif Latif, who handles equity investments at USAA. One theory holds that "if we are quicker to go into the slowdown, we are quicker to get out of it," he says.

Managers of U. S. international equity funds have racked up huge losses in the past few months, and investors have responded by pulling their money out. According to TrimTabs Investment Research, investors have yanked $48 billion from international equity funds so far this year, with $31.7 billion in fund outflows since the beginning of September.

Hang in There

On Oct. 6 overseas losses mounted amid a steep sell-off in Europe. London's FTSE 100 Index tumbled 7.85%, while Germany's DAX Index dropped 7.07%. The S&P 500 fell 3.85% after battling back from even steeper losses earlier in the day. In reaction, many expect Asian indexes to fall further when they open on Oct. 7.

For years, professional investment advisers in the U. S. have urged clients to diversify holdings by including some exposure to international stocks. Is it time to change this advice?

Experts on international investing say selling foreign holdings is probably a mistake at this point.

"It's a little late now. The horse is out of the barn," says Rob Lutts, founder of Cabot Money Management. "If you didn't act earlier this year, hang in there. It's going to be a rough next couple months."

Bargain Time

However, portfolio managers say many foreign stocks are now trading at bargain levels. "There are tremendous opportunities out there," says Aaron Visse, portfolio manager of the Kensington Global Infrastructure Fund. "Stocks are not trading on fundamentals. In many cases, fundamentals are really being thrown out the window."

Huntington's Matlock agrees, saying: "Fundamentals right now are not playing a role in this market." However, she isn't sure when investors will stop panicking and look at fundamental measures like earnings potential or economic growth.

"There's a crisis of confidence in the financial system," she says. "There is plenty of cash out there. It's just not being deployed.".

Nor are investors sure how well fundamental measures will hold up amid a global slowdown.

Hitting Poor Markets Hard

Of particular concern, several market experts say, are emerging markets like Brazil and Russia that are dependent on commodities. "The emerging markets are not all the same," Visse says.

However, all emerging markets have a common problem. In a time of crisis, investors "pull money out of high-risk areas," Lutts says. And poorer emerging markets are seen as much riskier than rich, developed nations.

The U.S. is suffering from a glut of housing, rising unemployment, catastrophic losses in its financial sector, high fuel prices, and weak consumer confidence. The odd thing is that, as the financial crisis spreads around the world, many investors seem to see the U.S. as a relatively safe haven.

第 4 章

UNIT 4

MANAGEMENT

• Text •

背景参考

"企业战略"是对企业各种战略的统称，其中既包括竞争战略，也包括营销战略、发展战略、品牌战略、融资战略、技术开发战略、人才开发战略、资源开发战略等等。企业战略是层出不穷的，最初人们所讲的"企业战略"，主要指的是竞争战略。1971 年美国的迈克尔·波特发表《竞争战略》之后，更强化了人们的这种认识。在迈克尔·波特的著作中，是把企业战略当作竞争战略的同义语来使用的，他说的企业战略都是竞争战略。军队从事战争，企业从事竞争。竞争与战争虽然本质不同，但也有一个"争"字，既然要参与竞争，那么当然就要讲究竞争战略，不能只是一味地拼人力、拼财力、拼物力。竞争战略非常重要，但不能代替企业战略，加强企业发展战略研究，在任何企业都是主要领导人的责任。

企业战略可以分为拓展型、稳健型、收缩型三种类型。

拓展型战略是指采用积极进攻态度的战略形态，主要适合行业龙头企业、有发展后劲的企业及新兴行业中的企业，具体的战略形式包括：市场渗透战略、多元化经营战略、联合经营战略。

稳健型战略是采取稳定发展态度的战略形态，主要适合中等及以下规模的企业或经营不景气的大型企业，可分为：无增长战略（维持产量、品牌、形象、地位等水平不变）、微增长战略（竞争水平在原基础上略有增长）两种战略形式。该战略强调保存实力，能有效控制经营风险，但发展速度缓慢，竞争力量弱小。

收缩型战略是采取保守经营态度的战略形态，主要适合处于市场疲软、通货膨胀、产品进入衰退期、管理失控、经营亏损、资金不足、资源匮乏、发展方向模糊的危机企业。可分为：转移战略、撤退战略、清算战略三种战略形式。优点是通过整合有效资源，优化产业结构，保存有生力量，能减少企业亏损，延续企业生命，并能通过集中资源优势，加强内部改制，以图新的发展。

金融危机的爆发，对于各个企业都带来了不同的挑战和影响，因此在金融危机背景下，企业战略的选择就显得更为重要。

Up From the Rubble: Post-Recession Planning

Organizations whose leaders look ahead to opportunities that will follow a grave crisis will have a competitive advantage when it's over.

By Kevin P. Coyne

Published: *October* 3, 2008, 11:18*AM*

The Strategist Column of BusinessWeek

At the height of the Cold War[1], government and military planners reached an interesting, if somewhat grim, conclusion that bears relevance for today's corporate leaders. **They concluded that while it would clearly be important for the U.S. to sustain less damage than the USSR[2] in any nuclear war[3], it would be equally important for the U.S. economy to regain its ability to function faster than the adversary's.** Whichever returned to a semblance of functionality first would be the long-term winner.

They thus developed plans to restore the basic payments system in the U.S. after a nuclear war. **At first it sounds crazy to design a plan to be implemented at a time when 98% of Americans would think the lack of a basic payments system was the least of their problems.** But the more you think about it, the more obvious it becomes that those planners were right. (Even though, thankfully, we never experienced an empirical test of their plans.)

CEOs and strategists[4] of companies would do well to learn a lesson from those Cold War planners. **Anticipating now what to do once the current disaster conditions clear-even partially-will be critical to any who want to emerge as long-term winners.**

POSTBELLUM FINANCIAL SERVICES

By way of example, take the epicenter of today's crisis: the financial services industry[5]. Bankers, investment bankers, and insurance company executives must undoubtedly feel that they are in the middle of the economic and competitive equivalent of a war. Like any generals, they cannot be sure whether the climax has been reached (in the guise of the meltdown of the last few weeks) or if the war will continue (as the recession that appears to be upon us).

Furthermore, the rash of bankruptcies and wave of mergers are already redefining the structure of the financial services industry. Investment banking has virtually disappeared as a separate industry[6]. The three largest banks—Citigroup (C), JPMorgan Chase (JPM), and Bank of America (BAC) are massively widening the gap between themselves and the rest of the industry.

In the midst of all this, CEOs and strategists at other financial institutions are sure to be in hunker-down mode[7]—focusing on short-term operations to avoid being the next victims. But as hard as it might be for them to contemplate—and even though they would (temporarily) be criticized for spending time on something "irrelevant" in the midst of a crisis—those executives need to carve out time to think about how their institution can act faster and more decisively than their adversaries when the war is over.

The first to recover a competitive and aggressive stance will look out over a landscape of widespread opportunities[8] and a period of unchallenged leadership while their adversaries remain hunkered down or absorbed in post-merger integration[9]. The big moves of the next 24 months will likely determine everyone's prospects for the next 5 to 10 years.

THERE'S NOTHING INEVITABLE ABOUT WINNING

This window of opportunity will exist in other industries as well. **The competitive industrial structures of the housing (including suppliers), automotive (including suppliers and distributors), airline, and certain high-tech and**

manufacturing sectors all appear to have "critical sensitive" characteristics, in which early recovery strategies could reap disproportionate gains that are unlikely to be reversed after economic recovery.

Five years from now, when the rubble has long since cleared, we will look back and believe it was "obvious" that certain players would recover, others would be the ones to act boldly, and so forth.

After all, we have revised history before. Haven't you heard people say that "of course" it was obvious Bank of America would recover from the LDC debt crisis in 1984[10], when its market cap[11] fell to $400 million, and First Interstate made a hostile bid? That "of course" it was obvious that NCNB[12] should buy bankrupt First Republic from the FDIC[13]—when in fact there were zero other bidders—thereby setting itself on the path to become NationsBank[14], which later took over Bank of America itself (but for $19 billion, not $400 million)? That "of course" it was obvious that Lockheed (LMT)[15] would recover from its government bailout? This list can go on forever.

The truth is that it is by no means obvious which companies will win. **But if we had inside information as to which management teams are sparing some effort today to act more boldly and swiftly than their adversaries when there is a pause after the disaster, it would be pretty obvious whom we should bet on.**

Kevin P. Coyne is senior teaching professor at the Goizueta Business School of Emory University and a co-founder of The Coyne Partnership, a boutique consulting firm focused on top management and board issues. He was formerly a senior partner at McKinsey & Co. He writes The Strategist monthly for BusinessWeek.com/Managing.

难点注释

1 Cold War 冷战

冷战是指美国和苏联及他们的盟友在1945年至1990年代在政治和外交上的对抗、冲突和竞争。由于第二次世界大战刚结束，虽然各方存在分歧和冲突，但对抗双方都尽力避免导致世界范围的大规模战争爆发，因此以"冷"方式进行，即

"相互遏制，却又不诉诸武力"。

The Cold War was a period of East-West competition, tension, and conflict short of full-scale war, characterized by mutual perceptions of hostile intention between military-political alliances or blocs. There were real wars, sometimes called "proxy wars" because they were fought by Soviet allies rather than the USSR itself — along with competition for influence in the Third World, and a major superpower arms race. (from ibiblio. org)

2 USSR: the abbr. of Union of Soviet Socialist Republics (前)苏维埃社会主义共和国联盟

3 nuclear war 核战争

核战争即使用核武器进行的战争。它以核武器为主要杀伤手段，其特点是战争的规模、突然性和破坏性将比常规战争空前增大。一般包括有限核战争和核大战。有限核战争是在一定地区内使用战术核武器的战争，或者是使用为数不多的核武器突击为数不多的军事目标的战争。核大战是指核大国及其联盟之间，以战略核武器的核突击起决定性作用的战争。

The possibility of using nuclear weapons in war is usually divided into two subgroups: A limited nuclear war (sometimes attack or exchange) refers to a small scale use of nuclear weapons by one or more parties. A full-scale nuclear war consists of large numbers of weapons used in an attack aimed at an entire country, including military, economic and civilian targets. (*From Wikipedia, the free encyclopedia*)

4 strategist 战略家、军事家

即能着眼整个战局，且拥有极强的宏观意识和长远的战略目光，并能全面详细正确地制定己方的战略方针，能合理分配使用己方所持有的力量与资源，从而引导己方获得战争的最后胜利的人。

A strategist is a person skilled in designing and planning action and policy to achieve a major or overall aim. (*From Wikipedia, the free encyclopedia*)

5 financial services industry 金融服务产业

金融服务产业作为一个为生产和生活服务的产业，既包括银行、证券、保险这些主要的金融服务行业，也包括信托投资、信用合作社、财务公司、融资租赁公司和典当业等行业。

The financial services industry encompasses a broad range of organizations that deal with the management of money. Among these organizations are banks, credit card companies, insurance companies, consumer finance companies, stock brokerages, investment funds and some government sponsored enterprises. (*From Wikipedia, the free encyclopedia*)

6 Investment banking has virtually disappeared as a separate industry.

投资银行作为独立的产业实际上已经消失。这里指的是在美国次贷危机影响下,像雷曼等的破产或并购现象。

7 hunker-down mode 沉潜待发的模式,保守的方式

That is to operate conservatively, for example, focusing on short-term operations to avoid being the next victims.

8 a landscape of widespread opportunities 充满广泛机遇的发展前景

9 post-merger integration 并购后的整合

Post-merger integration or merger integration refers to the aspect of an organizational merger that involves combining the original socio-technical systems of the merging organizations into one such newly-combined system. (*From Wikipedia, the free encyclopedia*)

10 LDC debt crisis in 1984 1984年欠发达国家债务危机

即20世纪80年代由墨西哥爆发而导致的全球性发展中国家的债务危机。

LDC (less-developed-country) debt crisis can be readily identified as Mexico's inability to service its outstanding debt to U.S. commercial banks and other creditors. (*http://www.fdic.gov/bank/historical/history/*191_210.*pdf*)

11 market cap 资本总市值

一种度量公司资产规模的方式,数量上等于该公司当前的股票价格乘以该公司所有的普通股数量。通常可以用来作为收购某公司的成本评估,其增长通常作为一个衡量该公司经营状况的关键指标。

Market cap is an abbreviation of market capitalization. It refers to the value or capitalization the market puts on a company. It is calculated by multiplying the price of the stock by the number of stocks issued. The market cap for a particular company varies from day to day. (*From wisegeek*)

12 NCNB 北卡罗莱纳国民银行

1988年,NCNB以13亿美元从联邦储蓄保险公司(FDIC)收购了第一共和银行(First Republic Bank)

NCNB is the abbr. of North Carolina National Bank. NCNB was a bank based in Charlotte, North Carolina, prior to 1960 called American Commercial Bank. It is one of the top banking industries today. (*From Wikipedia, the free encyclopedia*)

13 FDIC (美国) 联邦储蓄保险公司

FDIC为独立的联邦政府机构,1933年,美国通过银行法,联邦储蓄保险公司(FDIC)作为一家对银行存款进行保险的政府机构于1934年开始实行存款保险。在美的所有银行都要参加存款保险,在银行出现破产或危机时,存款之和小于2500美元的存款人都可以得到全额赔付。超过保险最高限度的存款人则得不到赔付,FDIC以此督促大额存款人选择银行时更加慎重,因为美国会对银行进行信用评级。19世界20年代和30年代的早期,成千上万的银行破产是此公司成立的直接原因。自从1934年1月1日正式营业以来,没有一家机构因为破产而损失一分钱的保险资金。

It is the abbr. of Federal Deposit Insurance Corporation. It preserves and promotes public confidence in the U.S. financial system by insuring deposits in banks and thrift institutions for at least $250,000; by identifying, monitoring and addressing risks to the deposit insurance funds; and by limiting the effect on the economy and the financial system when a bank or thrift institution fails. An independent agency of the federal government, the FDIC was created in 1933 in response to the thousands of bank failures that occurred in the 1920s and early 1930s. Since the start of FDIC insurance on January 1, 1934, no depositor has lost a single cent of insured funds as a result of a failure. (From fdic. gov)

14 NationsBank 美国银行

1998年时名称还是NationsBank的这家银行,以431亿美元并购BankAmerica,从而更名为美国银行(Bank of America)。

NationsBank was one of the largest banking corporations in the United States, based in Charlotte, North Carolina. In 1998, it acquired BankAmerica to become Bank of America.

15 Lockheed (LMT) 洛克希德-马丁公司

洛克希德-马丁公司是美国航空航天制造商,1995年由洛克西德公司和马丁·玛丽埃塔公司合并而成。是位居波音之后的世界第二大航空公司,从事航空和国防制造业，产品有 F-16、F-22 喷气式飞机，C-130J 运输飞机和高科技的拦截式、攻击式导弹，该公司约 70% 的收入都来自美国政府。

It is the abbr. of Lockheed Martin Corporation (NYSE: LMT). It is a global security company that employs about 146,000 people worldwide and is principally engaged in the research, design, development, manufacture, integration and sustain of advanced technology systems, products and services. (*From www.lockheedmartin.com*)

精华长句

1 Organizations whose leaders look ahead to opportunities that will follow a grave crisis will have a competitive advantage when it's over.

在巨大危机中寻求机遇的组织机构将能在危机结束后获得比较优势。

2 They concluded that while it would clearly be important for the U.S. to sustain less damage than the USSR in any nuclear war, it would be equally important for the U.S. economy to regain its ability to function faster than the adversary's.

他们总结，很显然对于美国在任何核战争中比苏联受的损伤要小都是很重要的，而美国快于敌国的经济复苏能力也同等的重要。

3 At first it sounds crazy to design a plan to be implemented at a time when 98% of Americans would think the lack of a basic payments system was the least of their problems.

首先，当 98% 的美国人认为至少他们的问题是缺少基础支付体系时，去设计一个在一段时间实施的计划听起来是很疯狂的。

4 Anticipating now what to do once the current disaster conditions clear-even partially-will be critical to any who want to emerge as long-term winners.

一旦当前危机条件明朗时，现在所做的甚至是部分的，对于想以长期胜利者身份出现的机构来讲都是非常重要的。

5 Furthermore, the rash of bankruptcies and wave of mergers are already redefining the structure of the financial services industry.

进一步来讲，草率的破产和合并的浪潮已经重新定义了金融服务产业的结构。

6 The first to recover a competitive and aggressive stance will look out over a

landscape of widespread opportunities and a period of unchallenged leadership while their adversaries remain hunkered down or absorbed in post-merger integration.

恢复竞争和积极状态的第一步就是寻找一个有着大量机会的领域和没有争议的领导时期，而其对手却仍处于保守状态或者被合并整合。

7 The competitive industrial structures of the housing (including suppliers), automotive (including suppliers and distributors), airline, and certain high-tech and manufacturing sectors all appear to have "critical sensitive" characteristics, in which early recovery strategies could reap disproportionate gains that are unlikely to be reversed after economic recovery.

房地产(包括供应商)、汽车(包括供应商和分销商)、航空、高科技企业以及制造部门所有的竞争性的产业结构都拥有"非常敏感"的特征，即其早期复苏战略能获得超比例回报，而这种回报不会在经济复苏后逆转。

8 Five years from now, when the rubble has long since cleared, we will look back and believe it was "obvious" that certain players would recover, others would be the ones to act boldly, and so forth.

在未来的五年中，当乌合之众早已明晰时，我们将反思并坚信诸如某些机构应当重建，另一些应有所作为等等是"理所当然"的。

9 But if we had inside information as to which management teams are sparing some effort today to act more boldly and swiftly than their adversaries when there is a pause after the disaster, it would be pretty obvious whom we should bet on.

但是，如果我们获得内部信息，如哪个管理团队能在危机暂缓时比其对手更努力并且决策更大胆迅速，非常明显的，我们就赌谁是胜利者。

理解练习题

1 How are the rash of bankruptcies and wave of mergers already redefining the structure of the financial services industry?

2 What is the first to recover a competitive and aggressive stance?

3 What's the character of the competitive industrial structure?

4 What would CEOs and strategists of companies do well to learn a lesson from

those Cold War planners?

5 How about post bellum financial services?

讨论

1 What do you think of "hunker-down mode" ? Discussion.

2 Have you ever heard people say "of course" to the deals according to the author? Give some examples.

3 Why does the author say that it is by no means obvious which companies will win?

4 Why has investment banking virtually disappeared as a separate industry?

5 What's your opinion of "if we had inside information it would be pretty obvious whom we should bet on." ?

• Extensive Reading •

Why limiting CEO Pay is a Good Idea

By Kathy M. Kristof

Published: September 28, 2008

Business Column of Los Angeles Times

One of the stickier issues to come up in the wrangling over how to bail out the imploding financial system is the question of how much money top executives at investment banks and other publicly traded companies are paid.

This is not an idle question. Chief executives at these firms are often paid tens of millions of dollars per year — so much that their compensation can actually cut into the company's earnings.

And during the continuing financial storms of the last several months, even CEOs who drove their companies into disaster left with fantastically rich severance packages.

But should executive pay be limited? And does it matter to you and me?

Where I'd normally report other people's ideas, just this once I'm exercising the columnist's prerogative to talk about mine. My answers are yes and yes.

I think executive pay should be limited to 50 times the pay of the average full-time employee — particularly for companies that want to participate in any government-funded bailout.

If the company's average wage earner takes home $ 20,000, the CEO can't earn more than $ 1 million. If the company exports all its jobs overseas, the wages of those employees are factored in.

The limitation is important because over the last two decades executive paychecks have gone from being generous to being piles of cash so large that they can significantly diminish per-share earnings (and, thus, stock price). At the same time, companies have outsourced vast quantities of work to cheap labor centers overseas — sometimes resulting in even higher pay and bonuses for the top dogs.

That's bad for both shareholders and taxpayers.

Why? Because a workforce that's paid a reasonable wage does a better job for customers, and thus for shareholders, than the bottom-of-the-barrel workers you get when you hire on the cheap.

Moreover, if employees are impoverished by stagnant wages, they can't buy what American companies produce. That's bad for the economy in the long run.

Opponents say that limiting compensation would hurt companies because the market for chief executives is highly competitive. Limiting CEO pay would hamper the ability to hire top CEOs and would make American companies less competitive, they say.

I'd counter that if we lose a few greedy, overpaid prima donnas as a result of this, corporate America will still survive — maybe even prosper.

Another thought: If top executives cut pension or healthcare benefits for the rank and file, they should be required to cut their own perks too.

After all, if a company can't afford retirement benefits for the people who most need them, how can it pay for multimillion-dollar annuities — or free doctor's visits — for execs?

Would limiting these perks discourage good people from taking the top jobs?

If a guy earning $1 million a year can't figure out a way to save for his own retirement or pay for his own doctor's visits, I think it's better that you keep this spendthrift away from a corporate balance sheet where he can do real harm.

As for severance agreements, how about if they're limited to one year's salary and bonus, except in instances when the company is being purchased at a premium price? After all, a year ought to be plenty of time for even a CEO to find a new job. Paying for longer provides an incentive for failure.

Finally, the company plane should be used for company business. These aircraft cost thousands of dollars each hour to operate, and if the CEO wants to take his family on vacation, he should have to pay the cost — not shareholders.

To be sure, these ideas may not eliminate every excess, nor would they necessarily fix what ails the economy. But I'm guessing that most taxpayers would feel a little less offended about their money being used to shore up failing financial institutions if they thought the game was a little more fair.

第 5 章

UNIT 5

MARKETING STRATEGY

• Text •

背景参考

企业在开辟市场时，应充分把握市场需求的变化，发挥靠近市场的优势，活跃于竞争变化快的领域，弥补市场需求空缺。特别是小企业，要充分利用经营机制灵活的特点，进入大企业尚未涉及的领域，集中力量参与那些大企业不愿涉足的批量小、品种多、利润薄的领域。采取这种策略，市场风险相对较小，成功率较高。

根据企业的经营条件采取措施，在某一方面突出自己的特色和风格，表现出差异性。事实证明，在强手如林的市场上，小企业只有从事有特色的营销方式才能站稳脚跟，从三个方面获得优势：在技术上，拥有专利技术、专有技术、精良的技术，使自身处于领先地位；占领特定的目标市场，融洽客商关系以增强企业的忠诚度；在市场竞争激烈的情况下，靠开发具有特色的新产品取胜，靠优质的服务、良好的企业形象取胜，靠物美价廉取胜。

在科学技术日新月异的今天，要注重把高新技术与小企业的灵活性相结合，进行技术创新。技术创新是小企业的生存之本，是企业赖以生存的物质基础，也是进一步发展的巨大动力。在物质上，创新能给企业带来丰厚的利润；在企业文化上，创新能使企业面貌一新，人才辈出。采用技术创新策略会使得拥有先进技术的小企业在世界范围内迅速崛起，成为技术革新的活跃力量。

要以一家大型企业为龙头，靠周围众多的小企业供应零配件的加工，搞专业化协作，在大型企业的庇护下积蓄力量，获得发展。在社会化大生产条件下，小企业依附于大型企业实行专业化分工协作也是一种必然的趋势。这会使小企业的产品开发专业化，能够保证销售渠道；依靠大型企业的技术优势和开发能力，突破小企业自身在资金、人才、设备等方面的制约，形成相互促进、协调发展的局面。

此外，由于小企业势单力薄，联合合作是增强小企业竞争实力的有效办法，还可以实现优势互补，发挥小企业的群体优势。联合合作有两种具体形式，一是松散式联合，该形式限于生产协作式专业化分工联合，参加联合的企业均保留自身的法人地位，在资本、技术等方面各自独立运作，企业间缺少法律约束力，不共担风险，也缺乏竞争力。二是紧密式联合，这种形式是企业间相互持股、利润分享、风险共担，其优点是各个小企业联合营销后，在资金、技术、管理上可以取长补短、优势互补，有利于形成规模经济效益，增强市场竞争力。

产品质量是小企业可持续发展的核心内容，必须认清小企业的发展是在高质量、高效益基础上的发展，要由过去单纯的产品数量管理转变为全面的产品质量管理，既重视产品的内在质量，又重视产品包装的外观质量，特别是产品的售前、售中和售后服务的质量。

参考文献

[1] 韩国光. 浅论小企业的市场营销策略. 2009 年 5 月

How Small Stores Can Lure Holiday Shoppers

With economists predicting one of the weakest Decembers since 1991, *merchants must put their best foot forward for top customers*[1].

By John Tozzi

Published: September 23, 2008

Sales and Marketing Column of BusinessWeek

Call it a customer service Christmas. Consumers are expected to rein in spending this year, and the retail climate favors big-box stores that can offer bargains. But because small retailers can't win price wars, experts say independents need to leverage their biggest advantage over the chains: personal relationships with customers and the ability to deliver superior service[2]. With some economists predicting one of the weakest Decembers since 1991, retailers that falter could face a cold winter.

"The independent and the small business person are fighting a much steeper battle for sales in a shrinking market," says Eugene Muscat, professor of management at the University of San Francisco. Unemployment reached 6.1% in August, the highest rate since 2003, and while gas prices are down from their summer peak, consumers still face high costs for energy and other essentials.[3] The spending boost from the summer's tax rebates has mostly petered out. With shoppers squeezed, the National Retail Federation[4] expects year-over-year sales to rise just 2.2% for November and December, half the average rate of the last decade, the group plans to announce Sept. 23. (Retail estimates exclude spending on cars, gasoline, and restaurants.) TNS[5] Retail Forward, a consulting and market research firm in Columbus, Ohio, predicts a 1.5% growth rate over the fourth quarter last year, while Deloitte[6] Services forecasts between 2.5% and 3% from November to January over the same period last year.

PURSUE THE WELL-HEELED

The outlook for independent stores is bleaker still, says Frank Badillo, senior economist at TNS. "As shoppers become more value focused, they're turning toward big-box retailers[7]," he says. Small retailers can bolster sales by targeting wealthier shoppers who are less price-sensitive[8] and may pay premiums for better service, Badillo says. **"Upper-income households often perceive of value in very different ways from lower-income shoppers."**

So what can independent retailers do to compete with their larger counterparts? Advice from experts follows:

1. **In whatever market they're targeting, small retailers need to court their best customers this holiday season.** "During the next three months they need to maximize the one-on-one personal relationships[9] that they have with customers," says Daniel Butler, vice-president for retail operations at the National Retail Federation. "That is the secret weapon that small independents have against big national chains. **If I'm savvy and communicate with my customers well, I can draw**

loyal customers into my store before they go into the national chains," Butler says.

One way to do that is through affinity discounts that encourage loyal customers to spend more, rather than trying to attract new business by cutting prices across the board, says the University of San Francisco's Muscat. "They're going to their customer base[10], and they're mailing out to their best customers targeted discounts to get them into the store. That's a lot smarter than putting a" 70% Off "sign in front of your store," he says. Through affinity programs, retailers can strengthen their relationships with their best customers and appeal to those shoppers' bargain-hunting mood at the same time.

2. **Beyond customer service, retailers need to keep inventories[11] lean to keep costs down.** Butler says store owners should be especially vigilant in refusing late orders and watching for overshipments to avoid having merchandise they won't be able to sell. In addition, small retailers can take a cue from large chains that display as much merchandise as possible on the floor, rather than holding inventory in the stockroom. "National chains don't have any inventory in stockroom," he says. "They want it to be out there where the customer is."

3. Likewise, stores should watch their staffing levels to control costs. "They want to be able to staff to the peak hours as much as they can," Butler says. That means mostly in evenings and weekends, as most two-income families[12] have little time to shop during the day. Businesses might decide to open later in the morning and extend hours at night to reach more customers without needing to staff more hours.

4. Retailers that sell both online and through physical stores[13] should coordinate their Web and brick-and-mortar strategies[14], especially in anticipation of "Cyber Monday," the post-Thanksgiving[15] is shopping day that's been deemed the online equivalent of Black Friday. Many people browse in stores the weekend after Thanksgiving and then make their purchases online. "If you have a Web site and do business online, you want to make sure you're cross-promoting your Web site with your in-store traffic and vice versa[16]," Butler says. Still, retailers may not be able to count on strong Internet sales. While TNS Retail Forward predicts Web sales will grow 9% this year, that's down from 19% in 2007 and the first single-digit growth rate since 1999.

难点注释

1 top customers 大客户、高端客户
high-quality clients, large customers

2 deliver superior service 提供优质的服务

3 Unemployment reached 6.1% in August, the highest rate since 2003, and while gas prices are down from their summer peak, consumers still face high costs for energy and other essentials.
八月份失业率为6.1%，创下了2003年以来的最高。尽管天然气价格自暑期高峰有所下降，但消费者仍然面临着能源以及其他生活必需品的高昂价格。

4 the National Retail Federation (NRF) 美国零售联合会
总部设在华盛顿。作为目前世界上最大的零售业行业协会，其会员单位既包括全美和其他50多个国家的著名的百货店、专卖店、独立业主、折扣店和大宗商品交易店，也包括100多个州级、国家级和国际性的与零售贸易相关的协会(组织)。同时，NRF也相应地吸收一部分主要为零售企业提供货物和服务的大供货商加入该会。
The National Retail Federation is the world's largest retail trade association, with membership that comprises all retail formats and channels of distribution including department, specialty, discount, catalog, Internet, independent stores, chain restaurants, drug stores and grocery stores as well as the industry's key trading partners of retail goods and services. (*from www.nrf.com*)

5 TNS: Transparent Network Substrate 环亚市场研究咨询公司
TNS是目前全球第二大市场调研和咨询公司，专注于快速消费品、汽车、IT、医药、金融等多个行业的市场研究，提供专业的市场分析和咨询。
It provides a user-transparent layer that enables a heterogeneous network consisting of different protocols to function as a homogeneous network. (*From Wikipedia, the free encyclopedia*)

6 Deloitte 德勤
德勤与普华永道、毕马威、安永一起构成世界知名的四大会计师事务所。德勤是“德勤全球”(Deloitte Touche Tohmatsu)的下属实体，是这家瑞士组织遍布全球的分支机构和会员。德勤全球在其国际化的战略指引下，在近150个国家和地区内拥有下属企业，汇集了12万专家，并致力于为客户提供卓越的专家服务

和咨询,其主要业务集中在四个领域:审计、税务规划、咨询和财务顾问。全球有一半以上的大型企业、国有企业、公共机构、本地重要客户以及成功的成长期企业都在享受着德勤的服务。

Deloitte Touche Tohmatsu (also branded as Deloitte.) is one of the largest professional services organizations in the world and one of the Big Four auditors, along with PricewaterhouseCoopers, Ernst & Young, and KPMG. (*From Wikipedia, the free encyclopedia*)

7 big-box retailers 大型商店,这里指大型零售商。

A large retail store whose physical layout resembles a large square or box when seen from above. A big-box store is characterized by a large amount of floor space (generally more than 50,000 square feet), a wide array of items available for sale, and its location in suburban areas. Big-box stores often can offer lower prices because they buy products in high volume. Also called super-center, superstore, mega-center. (*http://www.businessdictionary.com/definition/big-box-store.html*)

8 less price-sensitive 价格不敏感

9 one-on-one personal relationships 一对一的个人关系

10 customer base 客户群

The clients to whom a business sells products and services. The customer base is a relatively broad number of customers, with a smaller section of the base being comprised of repeat customers. (*http://www.businessdictionary.com/definition/customer-base.html*)

11 inventories 存货、库存

Itemized catalog or list of tangible goods or property, or the intangible attributes or qualities. (*http://www.businessdictionary.com/definition/inventory.html*)

12 two-income families 双职工家庭

The families in which husband and wife both work.

13 physical stores 实体商店

Stores which really exist, located generally in a fixed place, as opposed to virtual stores or web stores.

14 brick-and-mortar strategies 实体战略,与 online(在线) 或 virtual(虚拟) 相对。

15 the post-thanksgiving 感恩节后

The time after thanksgiving

16 viceversa 反之亦然

精华长句

1 The independent and the small business person are fighting a much steeper battle for sales in a shrinking market.

由于市场萎缩，个体企业和小企业主为销售而在萎缩的市场上进行激烈的争夺。

2 The outlook for independent stores is bleaker still, says Frank Badillo, senior economist at TNS.

环亚市场研究咨询公司的高级经济师弗兰克巴迪罗先生说，个体商店的前景仍然暗淡。

3 Upper-income households often perceive of value in very different ways from lower-income shoppers.

高收入家庭与低收入消费者对价值的看法不同。

4 In whatever market they're targeting, small retailers need to court their best customers this holiday season.

不管小型零售企业的目标市场是什么，这个圣诞节销售季，他们都需要努力博得最好的客户。

5 If I'm savvy and communicate with my customers well, I can draw loyal customers into my store before they go into the national chains.

如果我对我的客户非常了解，并且沟通到位，那么在那些忠诚的顾客走进大连锁店之前，我能够将他们吸引到我的商店里来。

6 Beyond customer service, retailers need to keep inventories lean to keep costs down.

除了客户服务以外，零售商还需要保持库存以降低成本。

讨论

1 What are the market advantages of small retail stores?

2 How different are the marketing strategies between small retail stores and large national chain stores?

3 How much is the developing space for small retail stores in the future international market?

• Extensive Reading •

Small Name in TVs Has Big Plans

By JASON TAN

***Published*: *October* 5, 2008**

World Business Column of The New York Times

TAIPEI, Taiwan — Buoyed by success in American stores, the TV company Vizio has dreams of worldwide expansion.

Vizio, which is based in Irvine, Calif., is considered a third-tier electronics brand behind better-known names like Samsung, Sony, Sharp and Panasonic.

But in terms of sales in the United States, the brand ranks right behind Samsung and Sony. It has grabbed almost 10 percent of the market by getting its LCD TVs into Costoo Wholesale, Wal-Mart Stores, Sam's Club, Circuit City, Target and Sears and pricing the TVs at less than the better-known brands.

"Put Sony and Vizio flat-panel TVs in a row and cover up the logos, and most people wouldn't be able to tell which is which," said Alpha Wu, chairman and chief executive of Amtran Technology, based in Taiwan, which owns a 23 percent stake in Vizio. Amtran makes more than 80 percent of Vizio's TVs, Mr. Wu said.

"The attractive price tags are made possible by a lower overhead," Mr. Wu said.

It is giving the company ideas. It plans to expand into Japan, China and Europe. In August, Vizio began selling a 42-inch LCD TV in Costco stores in Japan for 99,000 yen ($930). At a price at least one-third cheaper than Japanese brands, the first batch of 400 sold quickly.

Vizio will start selling TVs in Canada this year. It plans to sell TVs in China and Europe by 2010, Mr. Wu said. "We are a small company focused on what we do best. When we grow, we will slowly move into other markets."

The risk is that a low-price strategy may not lead to long-term success. Olevia, made by Syntax-Brillian, was pushing its way into the top sales ranks several years ago. It outlined big plans for greater success. It recently filed for bankruptcy protection.

Sony and Samsung heated up the competition this year by also cutting TV prices, with Samsung introducing a value line of TVs for the mass market.

The aggressive moves kept Samsung, based in Seoul, South Korea, at the top of the North American market in the second quarter, according to statistics from the researcher Display Search.

"Pricing strategy may be effective for a certain period of time, but it may not last long," said Peter Liu, a senior director at Samsung Taiwan. "Brand recognition is what counts."

George Chang, an analyst with Citigroup in Taipei, said that Vizio would lose attractiveness if first-tier brands cut their prices. "It will have to maintain the price gap to stay competitive."

第 6 章
UNIT 6
MODERN TECHNOLOGY

• Text •

背景参考

消费类电子产品在不同的国家以及不同的发展时期有着不同的内涵。我国消费类电子产品是指用于个人和家庭与广播、电视有关的音频和视频产品，主要包括：电视机、影碟机（VCD、SVCD、DVD）、录像机、摄录机、收音机、收录机、组合音响、电唱机、激光唱机（CD）等。而在一些发达国家，则把电话、个人电脑、家庭办公设备、家用电子保健设备、汽车电子产品等也归在消费类电子产品中。随着技术发展和新产品新应用的出现，数码相机、手机、PDA 等产品也在成为新兴的消费类电子产品。通过个人电脑及具有无线上网功能的手持式数字装置实现娱乐功能等被认为是消费电子业未来的发展方向。

消费性电子产业是一个不断创新的产业，从 20 世纪 90 年代后期开始，融合了计算机、信息与通信、消费类电子三大领域的信息家电开始广泛地深入家庭生活，它具有视听、信息处理、双向网络通信等功能，由嵌入式处理器、相关支撑硬件（如显示卡、存储介质、IC 卡或信用卡的读取设备）、嵌入式操作系统以及应用层的软件包组成。广义上来说，信息家电包括所有能够通过网络系统交互信息的家电产品，如 PC、机顶盒、HPC、DVD、超级 VCD、无线数据通信设备、视频游戏设备、WEBTV 等。目前，音频、视频和通信设备是信息家电的主要组成部分。从长远看，电冰箱、洗衣机、微波炉等也将会发展成为信息家电，并构成智能家电的组成部分。

在这种需求的驱动下，各制造厂商如索尼、三星、苹果、海尔、LG 等纷纷加大研发投入，在产品中融入了诸多新的技术，如功能复合化、无线互联、节能环保、高清化等。

然而，消费类电子产业面临的最大问题就是行业标准，如目前的 DLNA 和 WHDI 等，使得数字媒体和内容服务的无限制的共享和增长成为可能。

A Home Network Where Your TV Talks to Your Fridge

By KEVIN J. O'BRIEN

Published: *August* 24, 2008

Technology Column of The New York Times

BERLIN — Across the consumer electronics industry[1], leading players are revamping their audio and video equipment for a future centered around the Internet, a world in which televisions, stereos and computers — even dishwashers and refrigerators — can communicate with each other over a wireless home network.

Expanded lines of networked entertainment equipment will take center stage[2] this week at the Internationale Funkausstellung in Berlin[3], the largest consumer electronics convention in Europe, with 1,200 exhibitors and 200,000 visitors.

Sony plans to introduce plug-in adapters to enable some of its Bravia[4] television sets to connect to the Internet wirelessly. The Dutch consumer electronics maker Philips will demonstrate a line of stereo systems that can wirelessly tap into music stored on personal computers or laptops in other rooms, streaming music through the house. [5]

Pioneer, Samsung and Sharp will present flat-panel TVs[6] that hook up to the Internet[7], some with wires, some without. Hewlett-Packard's MediaSmart L. C. D. TV[8] will wirelessly stream high-definition video.

Some industry executives say the new focus on Internet content and wireless networks reflects a fundamental shift in home entertainment.

"The Internet is so massive," said Tim Page, technology marketing manager at Sony Europe. "So are the opportunities for electronics makers, content providers and consumers to get connected."

The convergence of telecommunications, consumer electronics and computing is bringing together a new set of competitors. Telecommunications operators, seeking to increase their revenue from data traffic, are actively promoting home Internet access[9] that is both easier and more sophisticated.

One way is through so-called residential gateways[10], boxes that combine an Internet router with a modem and software than can wirelessly shuttle video and audio among devices in a home. France Télécom has sold six million of its Livebox gateways[11] through 2007, according to Parks Associates, a research firm in Dallas.

Major online businesses also view the living room as a potentially lucrative new location for their services, with consumers turning to their TVs instead of PCs to reach the Internet. Google and Yahoo have said they will jointly produce software to make it easier to display Internet content on TV screens.

But the development of wireless home networks will require a shift in consumer thinking.

"Consumers really aren't driving the trend toward networked devices, the device makers are[12]," said Steve Wilson, an analyst at ABI Research in New York. "The companies are pushing this to try to build a new business, to offer new services. It is really a matter of getting the infrastructure in place."

While networked devices like Internet-ready TVs, set-top boxes[13], residential gateways and game consoles[14] are increasingly common, the truly networked wireless home is still a few years off, industry experts say. By the end of this year, 370 million homes worldwide will have broadband Internet, Parks Associates estimates. But only 5 percent, about 17 million, will have residential media gateways.

The technology already exists to enable many home electronic devices, including kitchen appliances, to communicate over a wireless network, said Alon Ironi, the chief executive of Siano, an Israeli company that makes video receivers for devices like digital picture frames. **The problem, Mr. Ironi said, is that most devices are unable to communicate with other manufacturers' products because of different technological standards.**

Although most major consumer electronics makers — Samsung, Sony, Philips, Panasonic, Pioneer, Sharp, Toshiba — belong to the Digital Living Network Alliance[15], a consortium whose common protocols ensure that their devices communicate with one another, that has not stopped some from hedging their bets. In July, Sony, Samsung, Sharp, Hitachi and Motorola joined the Israeli company Amimon in a new standards group for wireless communication, called Wireless High Definition Interface[16], which is working to produce a new HD video standard.

"What this means for consumers is that some people may bring products home and discover that they can't communicate with others on their networks," said Kurt Scherf, a senior analyst at Parks Associates. "We are just starting to see the first networked products roll out and a shakeout in standards is inevitable."

Still, manufacturers clearly think the appeal of a new information age centered on the living room couch will be strong enough to win over consumers who may be unimpressed by the early results. That is one reason that the former cordless telephone business of Siemens is starting to think about combining its phones with the Internet. Siemens sold 80.2 percent of the telephone unit, which makes Gigaset cordless phones, to Arques, a private equity firm in Munich, on Aug. 1. Although the transaction will not be completed until Oct. 1, the company is already considering plans to combine its phones with audio players and a wireless home network.

"Very soon, I don't think there will be any consumer electronics device on the market that isn't connected to the Internet," said Jochen Eickholt, the chief executive of the Siemens unit.

A version of this article appeared in print on August 25, 2008, *on page* C5 *of the New York edition.*

难点注释

1 consumer electronics industry 消费性电子产业,家电业

2 take center stage: to be in the spotlight 引人注目的中心人物,以某人为公众瞩目的对象

3 Internationale Funkausstellung in Berlin 柏林国际电子产品展览中心

它是欧洲及全球消费性电子、通讯及信息技术与产品重要国际展览之一,被称为消费性电子产品与市场发展风向球,展出当前消费性电子产品最新趋势。

The Internationale Funkausstellung Berlin or IFA (International radio exhibition Berlin) is one of the oldest industrial exhibitions in Germany. Between 1926 and 1939 it was an annual event, but as from 1950 it was organized on a two yearly basis until 2005. Since then it has become an annual event again, held in September. Today it is a world's leading trade show for consumer electronics and home appliances. It offers the opportunity to exhibitors to present their latest products and developments to the general public. In the course of its history, a large number of world innovations were first seen at the exhibition. (*From Wikipedia, the free encyclopedia*)

4 Bravia: Best Resolution Audio Visual Integrated Architecture 精晰影音杰作

它是索尼自 2005 年开始在大屏幕视频产品(主要为液晶电视)中使用的品牌名称。

5 The Dutch consumer electronics maker Philips will demonstrate a line of stereo systems that can wirelessly tap into music stored on personal computers or laptops in other rooms, streaming music through the house.

荷兰消费性电子制造商飞利浦将证实一系列立体声音响系统将以无线连接的方式把音乐存到个人电脑或者传到其他房间,使得音乐能在整个房屋飘动。

6 flat-panel TVs 平板电视

平板电视泛指非 CRT 类传统的显像管电视,包括液晶和等离子电视。

Flat-panel refers "a thin lightweight video display used in laptop and notebook computers and employing liquid crystals, electro luminescence, or a similar alternative to cathode-ray tubes. Also called flat screen". (*From The American Heritage Dictionary of the English Language, Fourth Edition Copyright* 2007)

7 hook up to the Internet 随时随地上网

Hook up is "to connect a mechanism and a source of power". (*From The American Heritage Dictionary of the English Language, Fourth Edition Copyright* 2007)

8 Hewlett-Packard's MediaSmart L. C. D. TV 惠普公司的MediaSmart液晶电视

惠普公司,一家全球领先的计算、成像解决方案与服务的供应商。致力于通过简单的信息终端产品、功能完备的电子化服务和永续运行的互联网基础架构来使科技与其所带来的利益达及个人和企业。

MediaSmart L. C. D. TV 是 2007 年惠普推出的高清电视产品,内置 Vista Media Center extender,允许用户将电视、照片、音乐和视频文件通过PC传递到电视屏幕上。支持JPEG, BMP, PNG, MP3, AAC, DivX (MPEG-4) 和 WMV等格式。L. C. D 即 Liquid Cristal Display 的缩写。

Hewlett-Packard is the world's largest technology company. And it is well know as a maker of personal computers. The company is the world's top maker of PCs and has been tied with Dell for the lead in the United States.

9 Internet access 互联网的准入

Access is "The right to enter or make use of: admission, admittance, entrance, entrée, entry, ingress". (*Roget's II: The New Thesaurus, Third Edition by the Editors of the American Heritage Dictionary Copyright* 1995 *by Houghton Mifflin Company.*)

10 residential gateways 家用网关,家用闸道器

A residential gateway is a home networking device. The term is generally used to cover any networking appliance used in homes. Multiple devices have been described as "residential gateways": cable modem, DSL modem, router or wireless router, network switch, wireless access point or any combination of the above. (*From Wikipedia, the free encyclopedia*)

11 Livebox gateways Livebox 家庭网关

Livebox家庭网关是 2004 年由法国电信子公司 Wanadoo 推出的,它将ADSLModem、蓝牙、无线 Wi-Fi 功能集成到了一起,家庭用户可以通过Livebox实现宽带接入、无线互联、VoIP、视频电话、邮件收发等多种业务,享受业务融合带来的便利。

Livebox is an ADSL wireless router available to customers of Orange's

Broadband services in the United Kingdom, France, Spain, Jordan, The Netherlands, Switzerland, Orange's Mauritian partner MyT and TPSA in Poland manufactured by Inventel. (*From Wikipedia, the free encyclopedia*)

12 Consumers really aren't driving the trend toward networked devices, the device makers are.

消费者实际上并不追逐网络设备的潮流,但是设备制造商却在追逐着。

13 set-top box 机顶盒

A set-top box is a device that enables a television set to become a user interface to the Internet and also enables a television set to receive and decode digital television (DTV) broadcasts. In the Internet realm, a set-top box is really a specialized computer that can "talk to" the Internet — that is, it contains a Web browser (which is really a Hypertext Transfer Protocol client) and the Internet's main program, TCP/IP. The service to which the set-top box is attached may be through a telephone line as, for example, with WebTV, or through a cable TV company like TCI. (*From SearchNetworking.com Definitions*)

14 game console 游戏机,游戏控制台

A video game console is an interactive entertainment computer or electronic device that produces a video display signal which can be used with a display device (a television, monitor, etc.) to display a video game. The term "video game console" is used to distinguish a machine designed for consumers to buy and use solely for playing video games from a personal computer, which has many other functions, or arcade machines, which are designed for businesses that buy and then charge others to play. (*From Wikipedia, the free encyclopedia*)

15 Digital Living Network Alliance 数字生活网络联盟

由索尼、英特尔、微软等发起成立,旨在解决个人 PC、消费电器、移动设备在内的无线网络和有线网络的互联互通,使得数字媒体和内容服务的无限制的共享和增长成为可能。其选择的各种技术和协议都是目前所应用很广泛的技术和协议。DLNA 既是其团体,也是协议本身。

DLNA (Digital Living Network Alliance) is a standard used by manufacturers of consumer electronics to allow entertainment devices within the home to share their content with each other across a home network without a complicated configuration process. The Digital Living Network Alliance is an international, cross-industry collaboration of consumer electronics, computing industry and mobile device companies. (*From Wikipedia, the free encyclopedia*)

16 Wireless High Definition Interface 无线高清解析介面

它是由 Amimon，Hitachi，Motorola，Samsung，Sharp，Sony，LG 等制定的全新行业标准。

WHDI is the new wireless High Definition video standard that will change the way people use Audio/Video devices in the home. WHDI's revolutionary video-modem approach enables top-quality and robust wireless uncompressed HD video delivery throughout the home, allowing consumers to connect any source in the home to any display. WHDI Special Interest Group was formed by Amimon, Hitachi, Motorola, Samsung, Sharp, Sony, LG Electronics. (*From http://www.whdi.org*)

精华长句

1 "The Internet is so massive," said Tim Page, technology marketing manager at Sony Europe. "So are the opportunities for electronics makers, content providers and consumers to get connected."

"互联网如此的巨大"，索尼欧洲公司技术营销经理 Tim Page 说，"同样的，电子制造商、供应商和消费者相互联系的机会也是巨大的"。

2 The convergence of telecommunications, consumer electronics and computing is bringing together a new set of competitors.

电信业、消费电子业和计算机业的汇集带来了一批新的竞争对手。

3 Major online businesses also view the living room as a potentially lucrative new location for their services, with consumers turning to their TVs instead of PCs to reach the Internet.

随着消费者以电视代替计算机上网，大部分在线商务也将起居室作为一个新的且潜力巨大的服务点。

4 The problem, Mr. Ironi said, is that most devices are unable to communicate

with other manufacturers' products because of different technological standards.

Ironi 先生说，问题在于绝大多数装置由于不同的技术标准不能与其他制造商的产品通信。

5 Still, manufacturers clearly think the appeal of a new information age centered on the living room couch will be strong enough to win over consumers who may be unimpressed by the early results.

尽管如此，制造商仍然想这种以起居室躺椅为中心的新信息时代的呼吁能够打动那些对于早期成果不为所动的消费者。

6 Very soon, I don't think there will be any consumer electronics device on the market that isn't connected to the Internet.

我相信，很快的，市场上将没有任何一个消费电子品不和互联网关联。

理解练习题

1 What do Sony, Philips, Pioneer, Samsung and Sharp do with their products?

2 Why do some industry executives say the new focus on internet content and wireless networks reflects a fundamental shift in home entertainment?

3 How do telecommunications operators promote home internet access for seeking to increase their revenue from data traffic?

4 Why will the development of wireless home networks require a shift in consumer thinking?

5 Kurt Scherf said, "What this means for consumers is that some people may bring products home and discover that they can't communicate with others on their networks." But why?

讨论

1 How do the consumer electronic equipment communicate with each other? Discuss.

2 Can you list any industries that belong to the consumer electronics industry?

3 France Télécom has sold six million of its Livebox gateways through 2007, according to Parks Associates. Why did France Télécom do so? Is it right in

the market mechanism? Give the arguments.

4 Why will Google and Yahoo jointly produce software? Is this win-to-win?

5 "Very soon, I don't think there will be any consumer electronics device on the market that isn't connected to the Internet," said Jochen Eickholt. Do you agree with him? Give the arguments.

• Extensive Reading •

THE FUTURE OF READING

Using Video Games as Bait to Hook Readers

By MOTOKO RICH

Published: *October* 5, 2008
Books Column of The New York Times

CARLSBAD, Calif. — When PJ Haarsma wrote his first book, a science fiction novel for preteenagers, he didn't think just about how to describe Orbis, the planetary system where the story takes place. He also thought about how it should look and feel in a video game.

The online game that Mr. Haarsma designed not only extends the fictional world of the novel, it also allows readers to play in it. At the same time, Mr. Haarsma very calculatedly gave gamers who might not otherwise pick up a book a clear incentive to read: one way that players advance is by answering questions with information from the novel.

"You can't just make a book anymore," said Mr. Haarsma, a former advertising consultant. Pairing a video game with a novel for young readers, he added, "brings the book into their world, as opposed to going the other way around."

Mr. Haarsma is not the only one using video games to spark an interest in books. Increasingly, authors, teachers, librarians and publishers are embracing this fast-paced, image-laden world in the hope that the games will draw children to reading.

Spurred by arguments that video games also may teach a kind of digital literacy that is becoming as important as proficiency in print, libraries are hosting gaming tournaments, while schools are exploring how to incorporate video games in the classroom. In New York, the John D. and Catherine T. MacArthur Foundation is supporting efforts to create a proposed public school that will use principles of game design like instant feedback and graphic imagery to promote learning.

Publishers, meanwhile, are rushing to get in on the action. Scholastic, the American publisher of the Harry Potter series, recently released "The Maze of Bones," the first installment in a 10-book mystery series that is tied to a Web-based game.

In advance of the publication of "Brisingr," the third book in the best-selling "Inheritance" fantasy series by Christopher Paolini, Random House Children's Books commissioned an online game. About 51,000 people have signed up since June to play and chat on message boards on the site.

But doubtful teachers and literacy experts question how effective it is to use an overwhelmingly visual medium to connect youngsters to the written word. They suggest that while a handful of players might be motivated to pick up a book, many more will skip the text and go straight to the game. Others suggest that video games detract from the experience of being wholly immersed in a book.

Some researchers, though, say that even when children don't read much text, they are picking up skills that can help them thrive in a visually oriented digital world. And some educational experts suggest that video games still stimulate reading in blogs and strategy guides for players.

To be sure, some of the experiments pairing electronic games with books will be little more than marketing gimmicks. But publishers and authors suggest that some projects may push creative boundaries, helping to extend storytelling beyond the traditional covers of a book.

The premise of Scholastic's series "The 39 Clues," for example, is that online players search for some of the clues themselves, encountering background stories about new characters as well as text and pictures about everything from the Titanic to the Iditarod sled-dog race, material that supplements the novels and inevitably entails some reading.

A New Narrative

A recent poll by the Pew Internet & American Life project found that 97 percent of children 12 to 17 play games on computers, consoles and handheld devices. But while video games may seem to have little in common with books, some see a clear connection.

"I think gamers and readers are looking for the same thing," said Rick Riordan, author of the popular "Percy Jackson and the Olympians" novels, who has written the first book in Scholastic's "39 Clues" series. "They are looking to be dropped into an intriguing story and to become a character in the story."

Still, avid readers who have compared the narrative arcs of video games with books sometimes find the games wanting. When Jacob Bagley first arrived as a freshman at Brown University, he was rapidly sucked into "World of Warcraft," an online game set in a medieval landscape where players collaborate to slay monsters and complete quests.

Mr. Bagley, now a senior, was so addicted that he sometimes abandoned friends in the dining hall to return to the game. But the story was never the attraction. Both the narrative and the characters, he said, were too simplistic, and he gave up "World of Warcraft" in his sophomore year.

Video games, said Mr. Bagley, 21, "certainly don't have the same degree of emotional and intellectual complexity of a book."

Some people argue that video games are an emerging medium likely to undergo an evolution. "I wouldn't be surprised if, in 10 or 20 years, video games are creating fictional universes which are every bit as complex as the world of fiction of Dickens or Dostoevsky," said Jay Parini, a writer who teaches English at Middlebury College.

Writers have also started to adopt the pace and perspective of video games. Quinn Clark, a video game player in Vista, a San Diego suburb, was drawn to Mr. Haarsma's novel, "The Softwire: Virus on Orbis 1," because of its similarities to some of his favorite games.

The novel is narrated by J. T., a 13-year-old boy who has the ability to burrow into a computer with his mind and fights aliens. His viewpoint mimics the behind-the-eyeballs feel of a video game.

"I felt like I was in 'Call of Duty 4,'" said Quinn, a beanpole thin 12-year-old, referring to a popular combat game.

Libraries Check In

Gaming advocates suggest that even if video games don't motivate more traditional reading, they have the potential to teach players how to absorb visual information and think strategically.

Inspired in part by such theories, librarians now stage tournaments for teenagers with games like Super Smash Brothers Brawl and Dance Dance Revolution. In the first half of this year, the New York Public Library hosted more than 500 events, drawing nearly 8,300 teenagers. In Columbus, Ohio, nearly 5,500 youngsters have participated in more than 300 tournaments at the public library this year.

"I think we have to ask ourselves, 'What exactly is reading?'" said Jack Martin, assistant director for young adult programs at the New York Public Library. "Reading is no longer just in the traditional sense of reading words in English or another language on a paper."

In some cases, librarians may guide young gamers towards other resources — including, occasionally, books. But critics argue that most children who play games at the library simply do just that. And games like Dance Dance Revolution, in which players follow dance steps on a screen, seem to have little to do with literacy of any kind.

At a gaming tournament at a branch of the Ann Arbor, Mich., public library earlier this year, more than 30 boys gathered in a darkened room, feverishly sparring in matches of Super Smash Brothers Melee for more than six hours. Most of them said they did not read much, and rarely checked out books.

Derek Hibbs, 18, a regular tournament player, said reading felt too solitary. "You can't say: 'I charge you to a reading duel. Go!'"

Researchers, who are just beginning to explore the cognitive effects of video games, have found that in laboratory settings, action gamers are better than nonplayers at focusing on tasks and ignoring irrelevant distractions.

Some gaming evangelists suggest reading feels too passive to youngsters who want the sense of power conferred by a control pad.

"Games are teaching critical thinking skills and a sense of yourself as an agent having to make choices and live with those choices," said James Paul Gee, the author of the book "What Video Games Have to Teach Us About Learning and Literacy." "You can't screw up a Dostoevsky book, but you can screw up a game."

Skeptics point out that psychological research consistently shows that skills often don't transfer from one setting to another.

Nevertheless, some educators argue that students may learn more by playing an active role in the simulated world of a game than they might by simply reading a book.

Such ideas led Lyn Lord, a social studies teacher at Kimball Union Academy, a boarding school in Meriden, N.H., to introduce students to Civilization, a role-playing game in which players build and lead cultures like the Aztecs or the ancient Romans through thousands of years of historical development.

Holly McLaughlin, a senior at Kimball who played Civilization as a sophomore in Ms. Lord's class, said that at first she failed at the game, choosing to develop culture and religion at the expense of roads and the military. Playing, she said, helped her gain a deeper appreciation for why leaders made certain decisions.

"Rather than just reading about it," Holly said, "you would understand everything about it, because you had built a network of roads yourself."

There is still little research on whether students ultimately absorb information better by playing games. "I actually think reading is pretty great and can compete with video games easily," said Mark S. Seidenberg, a professor at the University of Wisconsin in Madison who specializes in reading research. "So rather than say, 'Oh, books are irrelevant in the modern era because there are all these other media available,' I would ask shouldn't we be doing a better job of teaching kids how to read?"

Some gaming advocates suggest that video games may help with that. The reading that gamers do in instructional manuals, strategy guides or message boards, though often cryptic and more technical than narrative, might serve as a "gateway drug for literacy," said Constance Steinkuehler, an assistant professor in the school of education also at the University of Wisconsin at Madison.

For the past year, Ms. Steinkuehler has been testing this hypothesis with a group of teenage boys who play World of Warcraft.

Noah Tropp, 14, who participated in Ms. Steinkuehler's program for several months this year, regularly reads sites like gamewinners. com and supercheat. com. While looking for hints online, he read about "Death Note," a novel based on a Japanese video game. Over the summer, he read it.

Noah also wrote about the games and other pastimes on a group Internet forum. "I was so surprised because he does not like writing," said William Tropp, Noah's father. "I said, 'Why aren't you like this in school?'"

In one posting, Noah recommended "xxxHOLIC," a graphic novel based on Japanese manga cartoons.

"You should check it out if you get the chance," Noah concluded, "and it is a good book!"

第 7 章

UNIT 7

MODERN SCIENCE

• Text •

背景参考

神舟七号

北京时间2008年9月25日21时10分04秒，我国航天事业又迎来一个历史性时刻，我国自行研制的神舟七号载人飞船在酒泉卫星发射中心发射升空。21时19分43秒准确进入预定轨道。

9月25日，神舟七号航天员出征仪式于17时30分许在酒泉卫星发射中心航天员公寓问天阁举行。2003年和2005年，我国航天员杨利伟和费俊龙、聂海胜先后从这里踏上征程，开始太空之旅，两度实现了我国载人航天飞行的历史性突破。今天，我国航天员将第三次从这里出征，续写我国载人航天事业的新篇章。

这次神舟七号载人航天飞行的主要任务是实施我国航天员第一次空间出舱活动，突破和掌握出舱活动相关技术，同时开展卫星伴飞、卫星数据中继等空间科学和技术试验。这次载人航天飞行技术跨度大、任务风险大、航天员操作强度大、实施难度大、参试系统庞大。此次飞船发射是长征系列运载火箭第109次升空，也是继1996年10月以来我国航天发射连续第67次获得成功。飞船在轨运行期间，有关地面测控站和远望号测量船将进行持续跟踪、测量、控制，通过航天员生理遥测参数和回传图像及话音通信，了解航天员身体和生活工作状态。神舟七号载人飞船完成飞行任务后，3名航天员将乘坐飞船返回舱在位于内蒙古自治区中部的主着陆场着陆。

摘自《科学时报》（2008-9-26 要闻）

酒泉卫星发射中心

酒泉卫星发射中心又称“东风航天城”，是中国科学卫星、技术试验卫星和运载火箭的发射试验基地之一，是中国创建最早、规模最大的综合型导弹、卫星发射中心，也是中国目前唯一的载人航天发射场。

基地始建于1958年，海拔1000米，占地面积约2800平方公里，位于内蒙古阿拉善盟额济纳旗境内，现装配、发射场位于北纬41.118N，东经100.316E。由于地处荒凉，最接近的城市是其西南的甘肃省酒泉市，因而得名。

酒泉卫星发射中心组建以来，创造了中国航天发射史上多个第一：1960年11月5日，这里成功地发射了中国制造的第一枚地地导弹。1966年10月27日，中国第一次导弹核武器试验也在这里试验成功。1970年4月24日，长征一号运载火箭成功发射中国第一颗卫星——“东方红一号”以来，发射中心用长征一号、长征二号丙及长征二号丁火箭已成功发射了20多颗科学实验卫星。1975年11月26日，中国第一颗返回式卫星在这里发射成功。1987年8月，发射中心为法国马特拉公司提供了发射搭载服务，使中国的航天技术从此走向世界。1980年5月18日，中国第一枚远程运载火箭也在这里发射成功。1992年10月，发射中心首次为国际用户执行了发射任务，即利用长征二号丙火箭发射中国返回式卫星时搭载发射瑞典空间公司的弗利亚卫星进入预定轨道，获得成功。1999年至2002年，中国的4艘无人飞船从这里发射。2003年10月成功发射神舟五号载人飞船，将航天员杨利伟送上太空。2005年10月，神舟六号飞船成功发射，将两名航天员费俊龙、聂海胜送上太空。2008年9月，我国第三艘载人飞船神舟七号成功发射，三名航天员翟志刚、刘伯明、景海鹏顺利升空。

摘自新华网《中国的航天发射中心》

China Launches Space walk Mission

By DAVID BARBOZA

Published: September 25, 2008

Asia Pacific Column of The New York Times

SHANGHAI

The Chinese Shenzhou VII spacecraft[1] blasted off at 9:07 p.m. Thursday, carrying three Chinese astronauts[2] into space on this country's third manned space mission in five years.

The three-day mission is expected to include the country's first attempt at a spacewalk[3].

The Chinese government has spent billions of dollars in recent years building up a space program that it hopes will help China establish a space station[4] by 2020 and eventually will put a man on the moon, accomplishments that would certainly bring the country international prestige.

The launching of Shenzhou VII from Jiuquan Satellite Launch Center in Gansu Province, which is in western China, was shown live on state television.

At a ceremony before the launching, President Hu Jintao praised the space project's effort. "You will definitely accomplish this glorious and sacred mission," he told the astronauts before the launching. **"The motherland and the people are looking forward to your triumphant return."**

China sent into space three experienced fighter pilots, all of them 42-year-old men. One is expected to walk in space for 30 minutes on Friday or Saturday, according to the state media.

The three taikonauts[5] — the Chinese term for astronauts — plan to run tests in space and launch a small satellite monitoring station. They are carrying traditional Chinese medicine on board, in case of sickness, and their diet includes shredded pork sautéed with garlic and grilled beef with spicy sauce.

One astronaut is wearing what the state-run news media has dubbed "the most complicated, advanced and expensive suit in the world," a $4.4 million space suit[6] designed and produced in China. The spacecraft was launched by what the Chinese space agency calls the Long March II-F carrier rocket[7], which took the spacecraft into a low orbit, about 210 miles above Earth. **The mission, which is being covered extensively in the Chinese media, is another milestone for a country that got a late start in space exploration[8] but is now aggressively launching commercial satellites, putting humans in space and even shooting down aging satellites.**

"They have joined a very exclusive club; only the U. S. and Russians are members," said Roger D. Launius, a senior curator and expert on space history at the National Air and Space Museum[9] in Washington, referring generally to China's space program. "It's a great start, even though it's nowhere near what the Russians and the U. S. have accomplished with space flight."

Russia and the United States conducted their first spacewalks in 1965, and in 1969 the United States became the first country to put a person on the moon.

But Michael D. Griffin, the administrator of NASA[10], has repeatedly warned that despite the head start by other nations, the Chinese program is moving swiftly and could overtake American efforts to return to the moon by 2020. In testimony to the Senate last year, Mr. Griffin said it was likely that "China will be able to put people on the Moon before we will be able to get back." He added: "I admire what they have done, but I am concerned that it will leave the United States in its wake."

The Chinese government also hopes the national space program will aid the nation economically by helping to create technological breakthroughs that may someday be applied to computers or other digital equipment.

India and Japan are now aggressively developing their own space programs, creating some competition in Asia for space flight, and the Europeans have joined forces to explore space.

But China says its space program is speeding along, often with Chinese technology, helping establish the country as a technological power and bringing another dose of pride to the nation after the Olympic Games in Beijing this summer.

Because spaceflight requires large booster rockets and other sophisticated technology that often has military applications, national space programs are often veiled in secrecy, and cooperation among nations is complicated.

难点注释

1 spacecraft 宇宙飞船,航天器

A spacecraft is a craft or machine designed for space flight. On a sub-orbital space flight, a spacecraft enters space then returns to the Earth. It's always used for a variety of purposes, including communications, earth observation, meteorology, navigation, planetary exploration and space tourism. (*From Wikipedia, the free encyclopedia*)

2 astronauts 宇航员、航天员

An astronaut or cosmonaut is a person trained by a human space flight program to command, pilot, or serve as a crew member of a spacecraft. While generally reserved for professional space travelers, the term is sometimes applied to anyone who travels into space, including scientists, politicians, journalists, and tourists. (*From Wikipedia, the free encyclopedia*)

3 spacewalk 太空行走,太空漫步,是舱外活动(EVA)之一。

Extra-vehicular activity (EVA) is work done by an astronaut away from the Earth, and outside of a spacecraft. The term most commonly applies to an EVA made outside a craft orbiting Earth (a spacewalk), but also applies to an EVA made on the surface of the Moon (a moonwalk). (*From Wikipedia, the free encyclopedia*)

4 space station 宇航站,宇宙空间站

A space station is an artificial structure designed for humans to live in outer space. So far only low earth orbit (LEO) stations are implemented, also known as orbital stations. A space station is distinguished from other manned spacecraft by its lack of major propulsion or landing facilities—instead, other vehicles are used as transport to and from the station. (*From Wikipedia, the free encyclopedia*)

5 taikonauts 太空人

The word is a hybrid of the Chinese term "taikong" (space) and the Greek "naut" (traveler), or astronaut, according to the Concise Oxford English Dictionary. Another variation on the term is "cosmonaut", coined during the Soviet space era. Taikonaut was coined in 1988 when China started to train astronauts. It became well known in 2003 when China sent its first spaceman Yang Liwei to space in the Shenzhou-5 spacecraft. (*From WINDOW OF CHINA IN http://news.xinhuanet.com*)

6 space suit 航天服

"神七"航天员的舱外航天服,叫"飞天",重量120公斤,造价约3000万元人民

币,可靠系数 0.997,可以支持 4 个小时的舱外活动。"飞天"是中国研制的第一代舱外航天服,整体设计和各部件的设计、组装都是中国人自己完成的。就完成目前任务的能力而言,接近国际水平。(摘自新华网北京 9 月 25 日电)

A space suit is a complex system of garments, equipment and environmental systems designed to keep a person alive and comfortable in the harsh environment of outer space. This applies to extra-vehicular activity (EVA) outside spacecraft orbiting Earth and has applied to walking, and riding the Lunar Rover, on the moon. The first space suits were made by the Goodrich Corporation, then based in Akron, Ohio. (*From Wikipedia*, *the free encyclopedia*)

7 Long March II-F carrier rocket 长征二号 F 运载火箭

The Long-March II-F carrier rocket is a brand-new rocket used for the first time in manned spacecraft launching in China's space history, and among China's carrier rockets it is of the biggest launch mass, length and the most sophisticated systems. The rocket runs a full length of 58.3 meters, topped by an escape tower. Its launch mass is 479.8 tons, carrying capacity 7,800 tons, capable of sending spacecraft into the 200km-450km low earth orbit. (*People's Daily Online*)

8 space exploration 太空探索

Space exploration is the use of astronomy and space technology to explore outer space. Common rationales for exploring space include advancing scientific research, uniting different nations, ensuring the future survival of humanity and developing military/strategic advantages against other countries. (*From Wikipedia*, *the free encyclopedia*)

9 National Air and Space Museum 美国国家航空航天博物馆

The National Air and Space Museum (NASM) of the Smithsonian Institution is a museum in Washington, D.C., United States. It maintains the largest collection of aircraft and spacecraft in the world. And it is also a vital center for research into the history, science, and technology of aviation and space flight, as well as planetary science and terrestrial geology and geophysics. (*From Wikipedia*, *the free encyclopedia*)

10 NASA, abbr. of National Aeronautics and Space Administration 美国国家航空

与宇宙航行局

NASA是美国联邦政府的一个政府机构，负责美国的太空计划，在太空计划之外，NASA还进行长期的民用以及军用航空太空研究。1958年10月1日NASA正式成立。现在，NASA已成为世界上所有航天和人类太空探险的先锋。

Since its inception in 1958, NASA has accomplished many great scientific and technological feats in air and space. NASA technology also has been adapted for many nonaerospace uses by the private sector. NASA remains a leading force in scientific research and in stimulating public interest in aerospace exploration, as well as science and technology in general. (*http://history.nasa.gov/*)

精华长句

1 The three-day mission is expected to include the country's first attempt at a spacewalk.

为期3天的任务将包括我国首次尝试的太空行走任务。

2 The Chinese government has spent billions of dollars in recent years building up a space program that it hopes will help China establish a space station by 2020 and eventually will put a man on the moon, accomplishments that would certainly bring the country international prestige.

中国政府近年在航天计划项目上已花费了数十亿美元，希望能借之在2020年前建设一个空间站，并最终将人送上月球，这样的成绩将为中国带来国际威望。

3 The motherland and the people are looking forward to your triumphant return.

祖国人民盼望你们的凯旋归来。

4 One astronaut is wearing what the state-run news media has dubbed "the most complicated, advanced and expensive suit in the world," a $4.4 million space suit designed and produced in China.

宇航员所穿着的是完全在中国设计并生产制造的价值四百四十万美元的航天服，据国际媒体报导，"它是世界上最繁复的、最先进的也是最昂贵的航天服"。

5 The mission, which is being covered extensively in the Chinese media, is another milestone for a country that got a late start in space exploration but is now aggressively launching commercial satellites, putting humans in space and

even shooting down aging satellites.

目前媒体正在广泛报道的出征任务是中国的又一里程碑，虽然中国太空探索起步晚，但现在正在积极开展商业卫星发射，将人类送入太空，甚至击落老化卫星。

6 The Chinese government also hopes the national space program will aid the nation economically by helping to create technological breakthroughs that may someday be applied to computers or other digital equipment.

中国政府还希望国际太空计划能进行科技创新，并将其应用于电脑或其他数码设备，从而促进国民经济增长。

7 But China says its space program is speeding along, often with Chinese technology, helping establish the country as a technological power and bringing another dose of pride to the nation after the Olympic Games in Beijing this summer.

但是，中国表示其太空计划正随着技术发展而加速实施，有利于将中国建成为技术强国，并将在今年夏天北京奥运会后带来新一轮民族自豪感。

8 Because spaceflight requires large booster rockets and other sophisticated technology that often has military applications, national space programs are often veiled in secrecy, and cooperation among nations is complicated.

由于太空竞争需要强大的发射火箭和其他先进的适用于军事的技术，因此国家太空计划经常是隐秘进行的，并且国家间的合作也是曲折的。

理解练习题

1 Where and when did the Chinese Shenzhou VII blast off?

2 How did President Hu Jintao praise the space project's effort?

3 What about the astronauts' suit? How has the state-run news media dubbed?

4 Who conducted the first space walk? And who became the first country to put a person on the moon?

5 Why did the F. B. I arrest the physicist, Shu Quan-Sheng?

讨论

1 Discuss the significant of China launching space walk mission.

2 What are the possible reasons in your opinion that many countries give so much effort in the space exploring?

3 Why did Mr. Griffin say "China will be able to put people on the Moon before we will be able to get back" ?

4 Is it possible that space programs can be cooperated among nations? Why?

5 Using the internet to find more reports about China launching space walks mission.

• Extensive Reading •

Mars Weather Forecast: Snow

By KENNETH CHANG

Published: *September* 30, 2008

Space & Cosmos Column of The New York Times

The latest findings from the Martian Arctic offer more hints of a wet past but paint a very arid present, scientists reported Monday.

And in a prelude to winter and the demise of NASA's Phoenix Mars lander, snow has been spotted falling from the clouds above. As the Martian days shorten and temperatures drop, Phoenix's solar panels will eventually not be able to produce enough energy to keep the spacecraft warm.

NASA, however, has given a second extension to the mission, originally intended to last just three months and now in its fifth month. The extension will allow scientists to gather data until Phoenix's final day, anticipated to arrive in mid- to late-November or perhaps early December.

"We are trying to literally make hay as the sun shines," said Barry Goldstein, Phoenix's project manager during a news conference on Monday, "and really try to get the most of the science instruments in these last few days before the end of the mission."

The Phoenix landed north of the Martian Arctic circle on May 25, during late spring for Mars' northern hemisphere. Its mission was to explore whether that environment, currently dry, cold and presumably lifeless, might have been habitable in the past when Mars' axis was tipped farther over and pointed toward the Sun half of the time.

The mission has produced a trove of data for scientists to sift and ponder, but no blockbuster discoveries.

Instruments analyzing samples of dirt dug up by the Phoenix have now identified signs of clays and calcium carbonate, materials that on Earth form only in the presence of liquid water.

That liquid water is not there currently. A layer of water ice exists a few inches below surface, and the layer of soil on top of the ice is "very, very dry," said Michael Hecht of NASA's Jet Propulsion Laboratory.

Earlier, scientists had announced the presence of perchlorates, a class of chemicals that are toxic in high concentrations, although the implications for the possibility of life are unclear. The perchlorates could also explain the dryness of the soil, soaking up any moisture.

No organic molecules have yet been identified. "If there is any there, it's not very much," said William V. Boynton of the University of Arizona, lead scientist of the instrument known as the thermal and evolved gas analyzer.

The weather station, by shining a laser beam straight up and looking at the reflections, has spotted crystals of water ice — snow — from clouds 2.5 miles above the surface, although the snow has so far not reached the ground.

As the season moves to winter, the Phoenix will eventually be encased in a tomb of carbon dioxide ice. Mission managers said that after the spacecraft thaws out when spring returns, they will attempt to invoke its "Lazarus mode," but they doubted the spacecraft would revive.

Mr. Goldstein said the extreme cold would make electronic components brittle and prone to shattering. "The vehicle will probably not survive that," he said.

第 8 章

UNIT 8
WORLD POLITICS

• Text •

背景参考

朝鲜半岛核问题

朝核问题始于 20 世纪 90 年代初。当时,美国根据卫星资料怀疑朝鲜开发核武器,扬言要对朝鲜的核设施实行检查。朝鲜则宣布无意也无力开发核武器,同时指责美国在韩国部署核武器威胁它的安全。第一次朝鲜半岛核危机由此爆发。

根据国际原子能机构的资料,朝鲜于 20 世纪 50 年代末开始核技术研究。60 年代中期,在苏联的帮助下,朝鲜创建了宁边原子能研究基地,培训了大批核技术人才,并从苏联引进了第一座 800 千瓦核反应堆,此后,宁边成为朝鲜核工业重地。宁边核设施位于朝鲜首都平壤以北约 130 公里处,是朝鲜主要的核研究中心。宁边 5 兆瓦核反应堆属于石墨反应堆,于 1980 年动工,1987 年建成。这种核反应堆的废燃料棒可被用来提取制造核武器的原料——钚。1985 年 12 月,朝鲜加入《不扩散核武器条约》。90 年代初,朝核问题升级。2006 年 10 月 9 日,朝鲜在接近中朝边境的咸镜北道花台 360 米高山地下坑道内,进行了一次地下核试验。该核爆炸地点距中国东北边境仅 70 公里。

为使朝核问题和平解决,中国政府积极斡旋,于 2003 年 4 月促成有朝鲜、中国、美国参加的朝核问题三方会谈。同年 8 月,中国又促成有中国、朝鲜、韩国、美国、日本、俄罗斯参加的朝核问题六方会谈,并确立了通过谈判和平解决朝核问题的原则。截至 2008 年 6 月,六方会谈已进行到第六轮。2008 年 6 月 27 日下午,朝鲜炸毁了宁边核设施冷却塔。

摘自新华网

朝韩关系问题

2008年3月，韩国李明博政府一改沿袭10年的对朝“和平、和解、合作”政策，推行对朝“实用主义”强硬“新政”，朝鲜对此愤怒反击，朝韩关系变冷，朝鲜半岛局势出现紧张态势。

自朝鲜半岛分裂以来，南北关系的走向一直关系到朝鲜半岛局势的发展。2008年2月25日李明博就任韩国新总统后，推出了强硬的“实用主义”对朝政策，即“无核化、开放、3000”目标。朝鲜对李明博新政府出台的这一“新政”表示不满。4月1日，朝鲜劳动党机关报《劳动新闻》发表评论员文章说，这是“反统一的宣言”，给朝韩关系的前景造成严重障碍，将影响朝鲜半岛及周边局势。随着李明博对朝“新政”的出台，朝韩关系迅速变冷。3月24日，朝鲜通知韩方要求韩国常驻在开城工业园区南北交流合作事务所的韩方官员必须在3天之内全部撤离。

在朝韩经济合作遇挫之际，双方在军事上又起“硝烟”。3月26日，韩国参谋长联席会议主席金泰荣在韩国国会听证会上说，如果确认朝鲜具有用核武器攻击韩国的迹象，韩国军队将首先摧毁朝鲜的核基地。对此，朝鲜认为这是“先发制人的狂言”，无异于向朝鲜公开宣战。朝鲜方面表示，如果韩国不撤回其先发制人的言论，不进行道歉的话，朝鲜将中断两国间的对话和接触。朝鲜为表达对韩国的不满，3月28日试射了3枚短程导弹。韩国《朝鲜日报》还透露说，自李明博2月25日就任总统以来，朝鲜战机至少10次逼近非军事区和西海北方分界的上空。这是朝鲜同意停止核计划以来，半岛首次出现的军事对峙动作。

朝韩关系何处去，朝鲜半岛局势如何变，是国际社会普遍关注的问题之一。朝韩关系的发展，历来是坎坷不平的。每当韩国新政府上台时，朝韩关系经常要经过一段“磨合”。

朝鲜半岛分析家认为，朝鲜半岛局势与朝核问题和朝韩关系密切相连。实现朝鲜半岛无核化，为东北亚创造一个没有战争的和平环境，是确保朝韩关系改善和发展的大局。朝鲜《劳动新闻》4月1日发表评论说，朝鲜希望通过六方会谈实现朝鲜半岛无核化。在南北关系上，朝鲜表示将继续沿着2000年朝韩签署的《北南共同宣言》和2007年10月双方发表的《北南关系发展与和平繁荣宣言》所开辟的道路发展朝韩关系，谋求自主统一及和平繁荣。

朝鲜半岛的和平与稳定，朝韩关系的发展，关系到东北亚的安全与发展。目前，朝韩的对话大门并没有关闭。“对话总比对抗好”，人们希望双方重开对话，消除隔阂与对峙,共同探寻出一条能够促进双赢的南北关系发展道路,为朝鲜半岛的和平与稳定做出贡献。

摘自 2008 年 04 月 03 日 01:49 人民网 —《人民日报》

Mistrust and Hostility Between Two Koreas Shapes Life on an Island

By CHOE SANG-HUN

Published: *September* 30, 2008
Asia Pacific Column of The New York Times

BAENGNYEONG ISLAND, South Korea

Less than 10 miles from here, North Korea has amassed two army divisions, artillery and rockets — pointed directly at South Korea.

Should war break out, planes from the North would arrive in less than four minutes. And according to the South Korean military, the five North Korean naval squadrons[1] stationed in coves on the opposite shore would send out 360 war vessels, including 13 submarines[2], all of them swarming toward this island, the northernmost in South Korea.

For its part, South Korea's Sixth Marine Brigade, the Black Dragons[3], would move tanks and shore guns out of bunkers[4] here and unleash a barrage. Then 4,000 South Korean marines hunkered down in the hills would charge out.

"We will strike the enemy's side like a dagger," Lt. Chung Kyong-min, a South Korean marine detachment commander, said on a rare visit to his hilltop observation post.

This is the kind of mistrust and unrelenting hostility that Christopher R. Hill, the American assistant secretary of state for East Asian and Pacific affairs[5], will face when he crosses the inter-Korean border on Wednesday to try to persuade North Korea to stop its efforts to reactivate its nuclear weapons complex.

The tensions, a half-century old, pose an obstacle not only to disarmament, but also to the ambitious deal, announced on Monday, to import $90 billion worth of Russian natural gas into South Korea.

In Moscow, President Lee Myung-bak of South Korea, and his Russian counterpart, Dmitri A. Medvedev, sealed a deal that would send 10 billion cubic meters of natural gas in Siberia to South Korea over 30 years, starting in 2015. But they still have to persuade North Korea to let a pipeline pass through its territory.

Otherwise, they will have to opt for a more costly delivery route, like an undersea pipeline that takes a detour around the North.

Mr. Hill's trip to Pyongyang, North Korea's capital, at the invitation of the North Koreans is widely seen as a last-ditch effort[6] of the administration of President Bush in its waning months to salvage an agreement on nuclear disarmament[7].

That deal began crumbling in recent weeks as the United States demanded inspections to check whether North Korea was hiding any nuclear activities other than those at the declared complex in Yongbyon, north of Pyongyang. Without a North Korean agreement to allow such inspections, Washington refused to give the North the reward it had sought: removing the country from America's list of state sponsors of terrorism.

Calling the demand a slight to its sovereignty, North Korea has lashed out. It has removed United Nations seals on its nuclear facilities in Yongbyon and has threatened to restart, as early as this week, a plant there that can turn spent nuclear fuel into weapons-grade plutonium[8].

A challenge for Mr. Hill is whether he can work out a compromise verification mechanism that satisfies Congress in an election year and the North Koreans, who have turned more aggressive despite reports that their leader, Kim Jong-il, is ill.

Mr. Hill is the first senior Western official to visit Pyongyang since reports emerged in early September that Mr. Kim had suffered a stroke, prompting speculation over who is in charge in North Korea, which is armed with long-range missiles and enough plutonium to make about six nuclear bombs.

Secretary of State Condoleezza Rice[9] "believes it's important for Chris to go out to the region, particularly to go to Pyongyang, to get a sense on the ground as to what's going on," said her deputy spokesman, Robert Wood.

The United States suspects that besides its plutonium program based in

Yongbyon, North Korea has been pursuing uranium enrichment[10] and exporting nuclear technology to countries like Syria. The North says it never has — a denial Washington wants to verify through comprehensive inspections, including random visits and the taking of samples in all sites suspected of being involved in nuclear activities, including some undeclared military sites.

A senior South Korean government official close to nuclear negotiations, however, has indicated that Washington is working on a compromise that would offer a less strident inspection regime.

"You have to be intrusive at the end of the day," said the official, speaking on condition of anonymity. **"But you cannot achieve everything all at once. We can do this in an incremental way. We can move from the easy parts to the difficult."**

Mr. Hill had earlier sent North Korea a new, toned-down verification mechanism. **But the North did not respond and instead began reassembling its Yongbyon complex, part of which had been disabled under a nuclear disarmament deal struck in February last year.**

Mr. Hill said he would consult with his South Korean counterpart, Kim Sook, on Tuesday before crossing into North Korea through a border checkpoint north of Seoul, the South Korean capital.

"There is concern that Rice and Hill have lost momentum to work out an efficient compromise with North Korea, given Washington's preoccupation with the financial crisis and presidential election," said Ryoo Kihl-jae, a professor at the University of North Korean Studies and a member of the board of North Korea policy advisers for Mr. Lee.

Mr. Hill's strategy so far has been to nudge North Korea toward nuclear disarmament through a sequence of rewards intended to build trust. But he faced pressure from conservatives in Washington who insisted on placing a rigorous verification mechanism on the North, which has cheated before and has a tough road to persuade Washington that it would truly give up its nuclear weapons.

The degree to which such mistrust and enmity drive politics here is evident along the inter-Korean border, especially on this frontier island of 20 square miles.

Baengnyeong is the only place in South Korea where high school students and homemakers still join regular military drills with live ammunition[11].

North Korea has never accepted the sea border around this island. The two navies clashed in bloody skirmishes not far from here, in 1999 and 2002.

Last year alone, said Lieutenant Chung of the South Korean Marine Corps[12], North Korean gunboats violated the sea border 20 times.

Also, he said, planes from the North came within 25 miles of the border before turning around "in an intentional provocation to raise military tension."

But Maj. Han No-soo, a spokesman with the Sixth Marine Brigade, said there had been no unusual movement on either side since news emerged about Mr. Kim's ill health.

On this garrisonlike island, every strip of beach where enemy troops might be able to land is guarded by mines, steel columns and concrete walls. But the island's 4,500 civilian residents go about their business all the same, catching crabs and catering to tourists.

"We hear the marines fire up their guns in exercises so often and so long," said Kim Eung-gyun, 47, a Baengnyeong resident, "that we won't know if there is a war until an enemy artillery shell drops right at our feet."

难点注释

1 naval squadrons 海军陆战队

A squadron, or naval squadron, is a unit of 3-4 major warships, transport ships, submarines, or sometimes-small craft that may be part of a larger task force or a fleet. (*From Wikipedia, the free encyclopedia*)

2 submarines 潜艇

A submarine is a watercraft capable of independent operation below water. It differs from a submersible, which has only limited underwater capability. Submarine was shortened from the term "submarine boat". (*From Wikipedia, the free encyclopedia*)

3 Sixth Marine Brigade, the Black Dragons 第六海军陆战队

The black dragon is the name of the sixth Marine Brigade.

A brigade is a military unit that is typically composed of two to five regiments or battalions, depending on the era and nationality of a given army. (*From*

Wikipedia, *the free encyclopedia*)

4 bunkers 碉堡、掩体

A military bunker is a hardened shelter, often buried partly or fully underground, designed to protect the inhabitants from falling bombs or other attacks. (*From Wikipedia*, *the free encyclopedia*)

5 assistant secretary of state for East Asian and Pacific affairs 东亚暨太平洋事务助理国务卿

In the United States Government, the Bureau of East Asian and Pacific Affairs (originally the Office of Chinese Affairs) is part of the U. S. Department of State and is charged with advising the Secretary of State and Under Secretary for Political Affairs on matters of the Asia-Pacific region, as well as dealing with U. S. foreign policy and U. S. relations with countries in that area. (*From Wikipedia*, *the free encyclopedia*)

6 last-ditch effort 最后的努力

A desperate final attempt, as in We're making a last-ditch effort to finish on time. This expression alludes to the military sense of last ditch, "the last line of defense." Its figurative use dates from the early 1800s. (*from answer. com*)

7 nuclear disarmament 裁减核武器协定、核裁军

Nuclear disarmament refers to both the act of reducing or eliminating nuclear weapons and to the end state of a nuclear-free world, in which nuclear weapons are completely eliminated. (*From Wikipedia*, *the free encyclopedia*)

8 weapons-grade plutonium 武器级钚(Wg Pu)

Plutonium is a radioactive chemical element. The most important isotope of plutonium is plutonium-239, with a half-life of 24,100 years. Plutonium-239 is fissile, meaning that the nuclei of its atoms can break apart by being bombarded by slow moving neutrons, releasing energy, gamma radiation and more neutrons. It can therefore sustain a nuclear chain reaction after reaching a critical mass, leading to applications in nuclear weapons and use in some nuclear reactors. (*From Wikipedia*, *the free encyclopedia*)

9 Secretary of State Condoleezza Rice 美国国务卿康多莉萨·赖斯

She was U. S. Secretary of State from 2005 until 2009 under President George

W. Bush, after serving four years as National Security Advisor (2001-05).

10 uranium enrichment 铀浓缩

Enriched uranium is a kind of uranium in which the percent composition of uranium-235 has been increased through the process of isotope separation. It is a critical component for both civil nuclear power generation and military nuclear weapons. (*From Wikipedia, the free encyclopedia*)

11 live ammunition 实弹

Ammunition, often referred to as ammo, is a generic term derived from the French language la munition which embraced all material used for war (from the Latin munire, to provide), but which in time came to refer specifically to gunpowder and artillery. (*From Wikipedia, the free encyclopedia*)

12 South Korean Marine Corps 南韩海军陆战队

Though theoretically it is under the direction of the Chief of Naval Operations, the Marine Corps operates as a distinct arm of the military of South Korea, unlike most other "Marine" military organisations, which generally function as part of their respective national navies.

精华长句

1 This is the kind of mistrust and unrelenting hostility that Christopher R. Hill, the American assistant secretary of state for East Asian and Pacific affairs, will face when he crosses the inter-Korean border on Wednesday to try to persuade North Korea to stop its efforts to reactivate its nuclear weapons complex.

这是东亚暨太平洋事务助理国务卿克里斯托夫·R. 希尔周三穿越朝韩边境试图说服朝鲜停止努力重新启动其核武器反应堆时所面临的一种不信任和持续的敌意。

2 Otherwise, they will have to opt for a more costly delivery route, like an undersea pipeline that takes a detour around the North.

否则,他们将不得不选择一条成本更高的运送路线,如迂回绕过朝鲜的海底管道。

3 That deal began crumbling in recent weeks as the United States demanded

inspections to check whether North Korea was hiding any nuclear activities other than those at the declared complex in Yongbyon, north of Pyongyang.

由于美国要求核查朝鲜是否在除了平壤以北的宁边地区所发现的核反应堆外，还藏匿了任何的核武器，此次谈判在最近几周随之崩溃。

4 A challenge for Mr. Hill is whether he can work out a compromise verification mechanism that satisfies Congress in an election year and the North Koreans, who have turned more aggressive despite reports that their leader, Kim Jong-il, is ill.

希尔先生的难题在于他是否能制定出一个折衷的核查机制，不但能使得大选之年的国会满意也能让朝鲜人民满意，尽管报导说朝鲜领导人金正日正在生病，但朝鲜人民仍然热情高涨(对于重新启动其核武器综合体)。

5 But you cannot achieve everything all at once. We can do this in an incremental way. We can move from the easy parts to the difficult.

但是你不能一次就成功。我们可以循序渐进。我们可以由易到难。

6 But the North did not respond and instead began reassembling its Yongbyon complex, part of which had been disabled under a nuclear disarmament deal struck in February last year.

但是朝鲜没有回应，取而代之的是开始重新启动宁边反应堆，其中一部分已于去年二月根据核裁军协议被禁用。

7 There is concern that Rice and Hill have lost momentum to work out an efficient compromise with North Korea, given Washington's preoccupation with the financial crisis and presidential election.

人们担心，因为美国的金融危机和总统选举，赖斯和希尔在与朝鲜制定出一个有效的折衷方案方面已经失去了势头。

8 The degree to which such mistrust and enmity drive politics here is evident along the inter-Korean border, especially on this frontier island of 20 square miles.

尤其是在这个 20 平方英里的边境岛屿上，这种不信任和敌意导致的政治分裂程度在朝韩边界是显而易见的。

理解练习题

1 What has the North Korea done around Baengnyeong island?

2 What's the indicated meaning of Lt. Chung Kyong-min' s word on a rare visit to his hilltop observation post?
3 What pose an obstacle for importing Russian natural gas into South Korea?
4 What does the United States suspect of North Korea?
5 Why is Baengnyeong the only place in South Korea where high school students and homemaker still join regular military drills with live ammunition?

讨论

1 Why did Christopher R. Hill try to persuade North Korea to stop its efforts to reactive its nuclear weapons complex?
2 What about Mr. Hill's strategy?
3 According to the author's report, what did the South and the North do on the sea border around this island?
4 What the true meaning of the last paragraph?
5 What do you think of the two Korea relationship?

• Extensive Reading •

Envoy Pushes to Save Deal on Disarming North Korea

By HELENE COOPER

Published: *October* 1, 2008

Washington Column of The New York Times

WASHINGTON — The Bush administration's top envoy for North Korea, Christopher R. Hill, extended his trip to Pyongyang on Wednesday as negotiators from both sides searched for a way to salvage a nuclear disarmament deal that the White House had hoped to portray as a major achievement.

The administration is desperate to restore an accord that has been teetering on the edge since last week, when North Korea broke the seals that United Nations inspectors had placed on its equipment and said it was restarting a facility to manufacture bomb-grade plutonium.

State Department officials maintained that Mr. Hill would not offer substantive concessions but had proposed changes in what one official described as the "choreography" of arrangements meant to verify the accord.

Administration officials have acknowledged that the accord could collapse if the two sides do not reach an agreement this week. The Bush administration has already been fending off criticism from conservatives in Washington who argue that the United States should have extracted more concessions as part of the nuclear pact.

North Korea was supposed to be dismantling its nuclear reactor at Yongbyon as part of the agreement, and any resumption of nuclear work at the complex would violate the terms of the agreement, which was announced with fanfare in June and was followed by North Korea's public demolition of a cooling tower at Yongbyon.

North Korea's government has complained that the United States has not kept its part of the deal to remove the country from a list of state sponsors of terrorism, and instead has made new demands. Those include requiring North Korea to accept a strict and intrusive verification system before the United States would carry out reciprocal steps.

Mr. Hill is trying to find a work-around. One possibility, a senior administration official said, would be to rely more heavily on China, as close to an ally as North Korea has at this point, by giving it a more prominent role in verification efforts. Under one scenario, the official said, North Korea would submit a list of its nuclear sites to China, rather than to the United States; it would still have to permit inspections from American and Chinese officials.

Mr. Hill will continue negotiations on Thursday in Pyongyang, North Korea's capital, administration officials said. The reported ill health of Kim Jong-il, the North's leader, has also added uncertainty to the efforts.

In Seoul, South Korea, on Tuesday, Mr. Hill told reporters that an agreement on verification did not mean that the North would be subject to immediate inspections. "The verification will actually take place later on, but we need to know what the rules of the road are for verification," he said.

第 9 章

UNIT 9
TERRORISM

• Text •

背景参考

塔利班在普什图语中是"宗教学生"的意思,它的大部分成员是阿富汗难民营伊斯兰学校的学生,故又称伊斯兰学生军。塔利班是在 1994 年 8 月阿富汗内战不休、派系割据的背景下诞生的,它致力于建立"世界上最纯粹的伊斯兰国家"。塔利班的最高领导人为毛拉穆罕默德·奥马尔。起兵之初,塔利班只有 800 人,提出铲除军阀、建立和平稳定的伊斯兰政府的主张,赢得阿富汗人民拥护并且迅速壮大。1996 年 9 月,塔利班武装攻占首都喀布尔,并成立了临时政府接管政权[1]。

但塔利班政权未能获得国际承认,原因在于其统治政策粗暴,以及他们为伊斯兰教极端分子提供掩护。2001 年"9·11"事件后,塔利班拒绝将本·拉登移交美国,因此遭到美国及其盟国的军事报复,随后不久塔利班政权即被推翻,一些残余分子不得不转入山区,但依旧坚持作战和制造恐怖事件。

自从美国推翻阿富汗塔利班政权以后,塔利班就开始越过边境向巴基斯坦境内渗透,并在巴基斯坦西北部部落地区拥有了一定的势力。其中,斯瓦特河谷是其最坚固的据点。需要特别说明的是,巴基斯坦以前也有塔利班,阿、巴塔利班并不完全是一回事,两者相对独立,不存在直接的控制和被控制关系。不过,两者却有着千丝万缕的联系。他们的成员都以普什图族为主,成员多有血缘关系,交往密切。巴基斯坦塔利班派别众多,其中,实力最强的是马哈苏德领导的"巴基斯坦塔利班运动"。在英美情报部门的眼里,他们比本·拉登还要危险,被怀疑是暗杀巴前总理贝·布托，袭击白沙瓦美国总领事馆，制造伊斯兰堡酒店爆炸案等一系列恐怖袭击事件的主谋。在美国国务院的网站上，对马哈苏德的悬赏奖金高达500万美元[2]。

当前，塔利班主要通过制造恐怖事件和发起战争等手段与巴政府对峙，这不仅威胁到巴政权，而且使国内数百万平民连年饱受战争之苦，百姓伤亡惨重，并时常处于死亡和恐惧当中。考虑到政权稳定，同时亦受到来自美国等的压力，巴政府消除塔利班迫在眉睫，但由于美巴战略利益的不完全一致以及打击难度，巴政府不可能完全按照美国的意愿行事。此外，巴政府在重拳出击的同时，也从没放弃通过和谈实现停火的努力。

虽然巴政府为消除塔利班付出了巨大努力，但对塔利班的清剿收效甚微。国内不少民众指责巴政府措施不力，在一些战争区的民众在痛恨塔利班的同时也逐渐丧失对政府的信心，以致一些地区的部落成员不得不通过组成私人军队来抗击塔利班而寻求自我保护。

就目前来看，巴政府仍未找到解决塔利班问题的途径，因此，战争的结束还需要一个长期的过程。不知道还有多少百姓要丧生于战争中，还有多少百姓要流离失所、无家可归。

参考文献

[1] 塔利班到底是什么. http://zzrb.zynews.com，2007-08-02

[2] 北京青年报. 巴基斯坦塔利班为何难剿灭. http://www.ynet.com，2009-05-04

Confronting Taliban, Pakistan Finds Itself at War

By JANE PERLEZ and PIR ZUBAIR SHAH

Published：October 2，2008

Asia Pacific Column of The New York Times

PESHAWAR，Pakistan — War has come to Pakistan，not just as terrorist bombings，but as full-scale battles，leaving Pakistanis angry and dismayed as the dead，wounded and displaced turn up right on their doorstep.

An estimated 250,000 people have now fled the helicopters, jets, artillery and mortar fire of the Pakistani Army, and the assaults, intimidation and rough justice of the Taliban who have dug into Pakistan's tribal areas.

About 20,000 people are so desperate that they have flooded over the border from the Bajaur tribal area to seek safety in Afghanistan.

Many others are crowding around this northwest Pakistani city, where staff members from the United Nations refugee agency[1] are present at nearly a dozen camps.

"This is now a war zone," said Marco Succi, the spokesman for the International Committee of the Red Cross.

Not since Pakistan forged an alliance with the United States after 9/11 has the Pakistani Army fought its own people on such a scale and at such close quarters to a major city. After years of relative passivity, the army is now engaged in heavy fighting with the militants on at least three fronts.

The sudden engagement of the Pakistani Army comes after months in which the United States has heaped criticism, behind the scenes and in public, on Pakistan for not doing enough to take on the militants, and increasingly took action into its own hands with drone strikes and even a raid by Special Operations forces in Pakistan's tribal areas[2].

But the army campaign has also unfolded as the Taliban have encroached[3] deeper into Pakistan proper and carried out far bolder terrorist attacks, like the Marriott Hotel bombing on Sept. 20, which have generated fears among the political, business and diplomatic elite that the country is teetering.

Fighting on Three Fronts

In early August, goaded by the American complaints and faced with a nexus of the Taliban and Al Qaeda[4] that had become too powerful to ignore, the chief of the Pakistan military, Gen. Ashfaq Parvez Kayani, opened the front in Bajaur, a Taliban and Qaeda stronghold along the Afghan border.

Earlier this summer, the military became locked in an uphill fight against the militants in Swat, a more settled area of North-West Frontier Province that was once a middle-class ski resort. Today it is a maelstrom of killing.

At a third front, south of Peshawar, around the town of Dera Adam Khel, the army recently recaptured from Taliban control the strategic Kohat tunnel, a road more than a mile long that carries NATO supplies from the port of Karachi to the American and coalition forces in Afghanistan.

The new president of Pakistan, Asif Ali Zardari, spoke in New York during a visit to the United Nations General Assembly, about how the fight against terrorism was Pakistan's war, not America's.

But even as the gruesome[5] effects of the battles slam the national consciousness, there has been scant effort to prepare the public for the impact of the fighting. Public opinion has soured on Pakistan's alliance with the United States and has strongly opposed military campaigns that inflict heavy civilian casualties.

Hanging in the balance in the fighting is the allegiance of the civilians who have seen their homes wrecked, their cattle and crops abandoned, and their loved ones killed and wounded.

Pakistani Army commanders have said that in order to put down the Taliban, the government must win the hearts and minds of the Bajaur tribesmen.

Losing Hearts and Minds

But in interviews in the camps, and in villages around Peshawar where the displaced are bunking with relatives, many of the people of Bajaur say they are fed up with both sides of the conflict.

In the Red Cross hospital ward, two young brothers, Haseen Ullah, 5, and Shakir Ullah, 8, lay immobile on their hospital beds, their limbs tightly bound in white bandages covering what Dr. Daniel Brechbuhler, a Red Cross surgeon, said were shrapnel wounds.

The father of the two wounded boys, Hajji Sher Zaman, a relatively well-to-do used-car dealer in Bajaur, said he had no patience with the Taliban.

But Mr. Zaman said he was furious with the government for not holding anyone responsible for the killing and wounding of civilians.

"In Bajaur, innocent people are being killed as infidels, the dead cattle are lying on the road, the roads are tainted with the blood of the people who have been killed," he said. On return trips in recent weeks, he said, his village was "full of the rotten smell of dead animals."

"Why not target the real people, the administration knows where they are," Mr. Zaman said.

An Insurgent Sanctuary[6]

At a briefing at army headquarters in Rawalpindi on Monday, the military said it believed that Fakir Mohammed, the leader of the Taliban in Bajaur, had taken sanctuary in the neighboring Mohmand district. Another important commander, an Afghan Taliban, Qari Ziaur Rehman, had moved back to Afghanistan, it said.

From their side of the fighting in Bajaur, the Taliban have mounted a brutal show of intimidation, aided by money and deep support from across the border in Afghanistan and Mohmand, according to interviews with the displaced and with law enforcement and military officials.

Recently, the Taliban leader, Mr. Mohammed, stormed into a gathering of tribal leaders, arriving in a convoy[7] of 20 vehicles, said Habib-ur Rehman, a trader from Bajaur who now lives in a camp for the displaced in Timergara in the district of Dir, just outside Bajaur.

Mr. Mohammed, who is described by the army as one of the most skilled Taliban tacticians, told the tribesmen, "I'm here to get you to stop the meeting. If you don't stop, you will have a coffin over your heads,'" Mr. Rehman recalled.

The Taliban were well financed, some of the displaced tribesmen said.

According to the military officials at the briefing on Monday, many of the Taliban fighters come from Central Asia.

In Swat, the Pakistani Army has been fighting the Taliban for more than two months, and still the Taliban hold the upper hand[8], according to accounts from people who have fled the area.

Reports of Taliban terrorism are widespread.

Life in a Battle Zone

Many residents of Swat say they are exasperated[9] by the army-imposed round-the-clock curfew[10] that keeps them indoors listening to the scream of jets and the thud of artillery.

To increase the misery, the Taliban blew up the power grid last week, and when protesters gathered in the main street of Mingora, the police fired on them, killing six people.

More than 140 girls schools have been destroyed by the Taliban in the last several months.

In a typical technique to raise funds, the militants ordered the shopkeepers in the mall in the town of Matta to stop paying rent to the landlord and pay the militants instead.

"There is no light, no gas, no water, no food," Mr. Khan said.

The one hope in the gloom of war, said civilians and law enforcement officials, has been the formation of small private armies by tribal leaders, known in the region as lashkars.

They have traditionally served as a way of dealing with squabbles in Pakistan's tribal society, but are now being formed in some cases to stand up to the Taliban.

Forming Tribal Armies

In Salarzai, in the northern corner of Bajaur, a local private army has attracted several thousand anti-Taliban fighters, said Jalal-Uddin Khan, a tribal leader.

But whether the fervor of the tribesmen and their ancient equipment can be a match for the ideological zeal, modern weaponry and sophisticated tactics of the Taliban is an open question.

In other places, like Dir, just outside Bajaur, these private armies have pledged to keep both the Pakistani Army and the Taliban from entering their territory.

"Where the army comes, the Taliban come," said Sher Bahadar Khan, a tribal leader from Upper Dir. His community had organized a militia and persuaded the army not to put up checkpoints. The army was of little comfort because when the Taliban killed civilians, soldiers stood by as a "silent spectator," he said.

Closer to Peshawar, in the village of Shabqadar, where the Taliban have held sway for months, the local police organized civilians to join them in a display of force against the militants.

The police chief of North-West Frontier Province, Malik Naveed Khan, said he had encouraged the new police chief in Shabqadar to organize a "popular movement."

Last week, about 500 people, led by the local police chief, marched toward a fort controlled by the Taliban in Shabqadar, Mr. Khan said.

A 15-hour battle ensued, leaving nine Taliban fighters dead and 28 wounded, the police chief said. On the government side, one man was killed, and five wounded, he said.

难点注释

1 United Nations refugee agency 联合国难民署

It established in December 14, 1950. It is a United Nations agency mandated to protect and support refugees at the request of a government or the UN itself and assists in their voluntary repatriation, local integration or resettlement to a third country. Its headquarters are in Geneva, Switzerland. (*From Wikipedia, the free encyclopedia*)

2 increasingly took action into its own hands with drone strikes and even a raid by Special Operations forces in Pakistan's tribal areas.

巴军不断增加在巴基斯坦部落地区的空中打击和特种作战部队的搜捕行动来加强对激进分子的打击力度。

3 encroach 侵占,侵犯,蚕食

4 Al Qaeda 基地组织

It is a well-known Islamist group founded sometime between August 1988 and late 1989/early 1990. It operates as a network comprising both a multinational, stateless arm and a fundamentalist Sunni movement calling for al-qaeda al-sulbah (a vanguard of the strong). (*From Wikipedia, the free encyclopedia*)

5 gruesome 可怕的,令人毛骨悚然的,阴森的

6 An Insurgent Sanctuary 反叛分子避难所

7 convoy 护送,护卫,警护

8 hold the upper hand 占上风

9 exasperated 恼怒的

10 army-imposed round-the-clock curfew 军队实行全天宵禁

精华长句

1 About 20,000 people are so desperate that they have flooded over the border from the Bajaur tribal area to seek safety in Afghanistan.

约有两万巴基斯坦民众不堪战争之苦，不得不从巴焦尔部落地区越过边境逃难到阿富汗。

2 Hanging in the balance in the fighting is the allegiance of the civilians who have seen their homes wrecked, their cattle and crops abandoned, and their loved ones killed and wounded.

战争中，百姓的家园被损毁，他们的牲畜和庄稼被遗弃，他们的亲人遭受死亡和伤害，战争带来的灾难降低了百姓的信心和忠诚。

3 But Mr. Zaman said he was furious with the government for not holding anyone responsible for the killing and wounding of civilians.

但是，扎曼先生说，他对政府没能找到对百姓伤亡负责的人极为不满。

4 In Bajaur, innocent people are being killed as infidels, the dead cattle are lying on the road, the roads are tainted with the blood of the people who have been killed.

在巴焦尔，无辜的百姓被作为异教徒而遭到杀害，死牛躺在道路上，道路上沾满了死人的鲜血。

讨论

1 Many people are afraid of terrorist. Why do you think this is?
2 Why is it difficult to wipe out Taliban?
3 How should the Pakistani government deal with Taliban?

• Extensive Reading •

Terrorists and Spies, Weaving Their Webs

By MICHIKO KAKUTANI

Published: *October* 6, 2008

Books Column of The New York Times

John le Carré's latest novel, "A Most Wanted Man," is set in Hamburg, Germany, the city where Mohamed Atta and other members of Al Qaeda prepared for their assault on the United States — a "guilty city," in one character's words, which hatched this terrorist cell, and which, in the years since the attacks, has become a focal point for German, American and British intelligence.

It is in post-9/11 Hamburg that operatives from those three intelligence agencies play out a high-stakes game of surveillance and detention in this novel, and it is here that one illegal immigrant and terrorist suspect, and several earnest, liberal do-gooders, are caught in their nets of manipulation and betrayal. Although the story is enlivened by Mr. le Carré's intimate knowledge of tradecraft and his psychological insights into the reasons people become spies, informers and believers in a cause, the novel is flawed, like his 2004 book, "Absolute Friends," by an overly schematic narrative devised to drive home the author's contempt for the take-no-prisoners methods employed by the United States in the war on terror. As a result, the moral chiaroscuro and nuanced ambiguities that distinguished his cold war novels give way, in these pages, to a blunter, more predictable story line that lurches, at times, into sentimentality and contrivance.

As in many earlier le Carré novels, the central character of the story is a man struggling to come to terms with the legacy of his prodigal father. Issa, who turns up in the streets of Hamburg looking for refuge, says he's from Chechnya, and though he's "stateless, homeless, an ex-prisoner and illegal," says he plans with Allah's help to study medicine in the West. He will later claim that his father — a Russian colonel named Karpov, who he says raped his Chechen mother and abandoned her to her death — smuggled a large sum of money out of the country, and that he, Issa, has been told to contact one Tommy Brue, the sole surviving partner of a private banking house named Brue Frères, about those funds. He does not wish to touch a euro of that filthy money, he adds, but hopes that Brue can somehow help him obtain a German passport and residence permit.

Brue, it turns out, has father problems himself. It was his father who put the good name of Brue Frères at risk by recklessly setting himself up as a "banker of choice to a bunch of Russian gangsters." The secret money-laundering accounts he set up for the Russians were ingeniously called Lipizzaners — after the famous Viennese performing horses who have the odd distinction of being born jet black and turning white with age — and, in fact, it is the Lipizzaner name that Issa invokes when he finally meets Brue.

Issa's movements are being tracked by German authorities — some of whom assert that he is "an Islamist Russian criminal with a long record of convictions for militant actions," a dangerous man who has escaped from prison and had himself smuggled into Germany. Meanwhile, several well-meaning Hamburg residents have set about trying to help Issa. Instead of seeing a dangerous militant, they see a traumatized young man, still reeling from the torture he was subjected to in prison — a sensitive youth, who aspires to become a doctor and who likes to listen to Tchaikovsky.

Leyla, a Turkish émigré, and her son, Melik, give Issa temporary refuge in their apartment, although they fear that their act of kindness — or gullibility — will compromise their chances for obtaining German citizenship. And a young lawyer named Annabel Richter, who works for an organization called Sanctuary North — "A Charitable Christian Foundation for the protection of stateless and displaced persons in the Region of North Germany" — takes him on as a client and presses his case to Brue.

Predictably enough, a series of emotional entanglements complicates matters further. Brue finds himself drawn to Annabel, who vaguely reminds him of his estranged daughter and, seduced by her idealism, he becomes obsessed with the idea of expiating the sins of his father in the service of a humanitarian cause. At the same time, Annabel — whose work underscores her rebellion against her wealthy, Establishment family — finds herself drawn to Issa, who begins to fantasize about marrying her one day.

As for the German operatives monitoring Issa's case, they soon find themselves clashing with other members of Berlin's "espiocracy," as well as

British and American intelligence interests, as the case against this illegal immigrant grows increasingly complex. Was the identification of Issa as a member of a violent militant group obtained from a supposed Chechen jihadist through torture — and therefore possibly false? Is Abdullah, an eminent Islamic philosopher living in Hamburg and renowned for his charitable works, actually funneling money to terrorists, and will Issa, who wants to donate his father's dirty money to those charities, become a tool of the intelligence agents who want to use him to entrap the religious leader?

Mr. le Carré orchestrates these developments smoothly but glibly — like a thriller screenwriter on automatic pilot. And while his portraits of Annabel, Brue and some of the German intelligence operatives are emotionally detailed, Issa and Abdullah remain flimsy stick figures — more symbols than human beings.

For that matter, Mr. le Carré's contempt for the United States' post-9/11 approach to the war on terror not only makes for a story told in blacks and whites — with none of the grays that distinguished his famous Smiley novels — but also results in an ending that the reader can see looming a mile off.

第 10 章

UNIT 10

SOCIAL LIFE

• Text •

背景参考

进入 21 世纪以来，人口年龄结构的老化是世界人口发展的基本趋势，人口老龄化已日益成为世界各国关注的重大社会问题。如何解决人口老龄化及其所带来的问题，受到世界各国的普遍关注。

据联合国统计，目前全球人口中 60 岁以上的老年人占 1/10，这一比例在 2050 年将达到 1/5，世界人口的老龄化趋势正在加快。尤其是中国，是世界老龄人口最多的国家，据预测，到本世纪中叶，我国老年人口将超过 4 亿，占总人口的 1/4 左右，大大超过世界的平均水平[1]。随着老龄社会的到来，人们应该更加关注这一群体。

老年人是一个特殊的群体，很多老人在退休后，角色发生变化，生活圈子变小，生活目标亦发生转移。同时，伴随着身体机能上的衰退，比如视力、听觉等的衰退，一些老人可能存在情绪障碍，容易产生失落感、孤独感、焦虑感，缺乏安全感等。

面对老年人的这些特性，在与老人沟通时，要特别注意这方面的问题。沟通是一个双向的过程，它使两个人通过传达及接收信息互相了解。

在与他人沟通时，特别是与老人沟通时，人们从不同角度提出了沟通时的注意事项[2]。

要设身处地从老人的角度去看和感受事物，并且合理地传达信息，使老人感觉被理解和接受，这将给老人极大的支持。

用坦诚的态度与老人交往，使他们感受到一种真挚的关心。老人大部分缺乏安全感,希望得到别人的关怀及接纳,要以爱心及体谅去接纳他们。

老人时常会感到自己无用,容易产生自卑感,要给予其尊重和支持,增强其自尊心,提升其自我形象。

很多老人比较被动,自信心低,对人有戒心,因此要积极主动地接触他们,使他们感到被关心。

沟通中极为重要的一个方面是语言的运用,语言交流具有特殊的魅力,准确而亲切的语言是增进相互感情的重要手段。特别是在医院里,语言可治病亦可致病,医护人员的语言对患者可产生重要的作用,对病情的好转和康复有极大的帮助[3]。

在本章所选的第一篇文章中,作者对与老人沟通中的语言运用方面进行了探索,引入"老人语言"的概念,并着眼于现今学者们对"老人语言"方面做出的实验研究,以及从老人讲述的亲身经历中,让人们了解"宝贝"、"甜心"这些用语对老人来说的不同含义。

参考文献

[1] 陈庆修.企业积极应对社会老龄化问题.中外企业文化,2005(5):11.

[2] 孔颖秀.护患沟通的方式和技巧.中国社区医师,2008(13):187.

[3] 王培才.浅议沟通方式对沟通质量的影响.商场现代化,2007(12):123.

In 'Sweetie' and 'Dear', a Hurt for the Elderly

By JOHN LELAND

Published: *October* 6, 2008

U.S. Column of The New York Times

Professionals call it elderspeak[1], the sweetly belittling form of address that has always rankled older people: the doctor who talks to their child rather than to them about their health; the store clerk who assumes that an older person does not know how to work a computer, or needs to be addressed slowly or in a loud voice. Then there are those who address any elderly person as "dear."

"People think they're being nice," said Elvira, 83, of Dublin, Calif., "**but when I hear it, it raises my hackles.**"

Now studies are finding that the insults can have health consequences, especially if people mutely accept the attitudes behind them, said Becca Levy, an associate professor of epidemiology and psychology at Yale University, who studies the health effects of such messages on elderly people.

"Those little insults can lead to more negative images of aging[2]," Dr. Levy said. "And those who have more negative images of aging have worse functional health over time, including lower rates of survival."

In a long-term survey of 660 people over age 50 in a small Ohio town, Dr. Levy and her fellow researchers found that those who had positive perceptions of aging lived an average of 7.5 years longer, a bigger increase than that associated with exercising or not smoking. The findings held up even when the researchers controlled for differences in the participants' health conditions.

In her forthcoming study, Dr. Levy found that older people exposed to negative images of aging, including words like "forgetful," "feeble" and "shaky," performed significantly worse on memory and balance tests; in previous experiments, they also showed higher levels of stress.

Despite such research, the worst offenders are often health care workers, said Kristine Williams, a nurse gerontologist and associate professor at the University of Kansas School of Nursing.

To study the effects of elderspeak on people with mild to moderate dementia, Dr. Williams and a team of researchers videotaped interactions in a nursing home between 20 residents and staff members. They found that when nurses used phrases like "good girl" or "How are we feeling?" patients were more aggressive and less cooperative or receptive to care. **If addressed as infants, some showed their irritation by grimacing, screaming or refusing to do what staff members asked of them.**

The researchers, who will publish their findings in The American Journal of Alzheimer's Disease[3]. and Other Dementias, concluded that elderspeak sent a message that the patient was incompetent and "begins a negative downward spiral for older persons, who react with decreased self-esteem, depression[4], withdrawal and the assumption of dependent behaviors."

Dr. Williams said health care workers often thought that using words like "dear" or "sweetie" conveyed that they cared and made them easier to understand. "But they don't realize the implications," she said, "that it's also giving messages to older adults that they're incompetent."

"The main task for a person with Alzheimer's is to maintain a sense of self or personhood[5]," Dr. Williams said. "If you know you're losing your cognitive abilities[6] and trying to maintain your personhood, and someone talks to you like a baby, it's upsetting to you."

For people without cognitive problems, elderspeak can sometimes make them livid[7]. When Sarah Plummer's pharmacy changed her monthly prescription for cancer drugs from a vial to a contraption she could not open, she said, the pharmacist[8] explained that the packaging was intended to help her remember her daily dose.

"I exploded," Ms. Plummer wrote to a New York Times blog, The New Old Age, which asked readers about how they were treated in their daily life.

"Who says I don't take my medicine as prescribed?" wrote Ms. Plummer, 61, who lives in Champaign, Ill. "I am alive right now because I take these pills! What am I supposed to do? Hold it with vice grips and cut it with a hack saw?'"

She added, "I believed my dignity and integrity were being assaulted."

Health care workers are often not trained to avoid elderspeak, said Vicki Rosebrook, the executive director of the Macklin Intergenerational Institute in Findlay, Ohio, a combined facility for elderly people and children that is part of a retirement community.

Dr. Rosebrook said that even in her facility, "we have 300 elders who are 'sweetie'd' here. Our kids talk to elders with more respect than some of our professional care providers."

She said she considered elderspeak a form of bullying. "It's talking down to them," she said. "We do it to children so well. And it's natural for the sandwich generation[9], since they address children that way."

Not all older people object to being called sweetie or dear, and some, like Jan Rowell, 61, of West Linn, Ore., say they appreciate the underlying warmth.

"We're all reaching across the chasm," Ms. Rowell said. "If someone calls us sweetie or honey, it's not diminishing us; it's just their way to connect, in a positive way."

She added, "What would reinforce negative stereotypes is the idea that old people are filled with pet peeves, taking offense at innocent attempts to be friendly."

But Ellen Kirschman, 68, a police psychologist in Northern California, said she objected to people calling her "young lady," which she called "mocking and disingenuous[10]." She added: "As I get older, I don't want to be recognized for my age. I want to be recognized for my accomplishments, for my wisdom."

Bea Howard, 77, a retired teacher in Berkeley, Calif., said she objected less to the ways people addressed her than to their ignoring her altogether. At recent meals with a younger friend, Ms. Howard said, the restaurant's staff spoke only to the friend.

"They ask my friend, 'How are you; how are you feeling?' just turning on the charm to my partner," Ms. Howard said. "Then they ask for my order. I say: 'I feel you're ignoring me; I'm at this table, too.' And they immediately deny it. They say, no, not at all. And they may not even know they're doing it."

Dr. Levy of Yale said that even among professionals, there appeared to be little movement to reduce elderspeak. Words like "dear," she said, have a life of their own. **"It's harder to change," Dr. Levy said, "because people spend so much of their lives observing it without having a stake in it, not realizing it's belittling to call someone that."**

In the meantime, people who are offended might do well to follow the advice of Warren Cassell of Portland, Ore., who said it irritated him when "teenage store clerks and about 95 percent of the rest of society" called him by his first name. "It's the faux familiarity," said Mr. Cassell, 78.

But he mostly shrugs it off, he said. "I'm irked by it, but I can't think about it that much," he said. "There are too many more important things to think about."

难点注释

1 elderspeak 老人语言

Elderspeak has been assumed to be an accommodation to the perceived communication needs of older adults as it involves a slow rate of speaking, simplified syntax, vocabulary restrictions, and exaggerated prosody. (*Kemper, Susan. Elderspeak, http://adsabs.harvard.edu*)

2 negative images of aging 衰老的负面形象

3 Alzheimer's Disease 失智症、老年痴呆症、阿尔茨海默氏病

阿尔茨海默氏病(AD)是一种由于大脑神经细胞死亡而造成的神经性疾病。AD的发生是典型的渐进过程,其最初症状可能会被认为是年迈或普通的健忘。随着病情的发展,认知能力包括决策能力和日常活动能力将逐渐丧失,同时可能出现性情改变以及行为困难的情况。在晚期,AD会导致失智并最终导致死亡。

Alzheimer's disease is a brain disorder named for German physician Alois Alzheimer, who first described it in 1906. It destroys brain cells, causing problems with memory, thinking and behavior severe enough to affect work, lifelong hobbies or social life. Alzheimer's gets worse over time, and it is fatal. (*www.alz.org*)

4 depression 抑郁、沮丧、消沉

5 personhood 人格

6 cognitive abilities 认知能力

7 livid 生气的、铅色的、(被打得)青紫色的

8 pharmacist 药剂师

Pharmacists are health professionals who practice the science of pharmacy.

9 sandwich generation 三明治的一代(指必须同时抚养孩子和照顾老人的中年父母)

10 mocking and disingenuous 被嘲弄且无诚意

精华长句

1 Professionals call it elderspeak, the sweetly belittling form of address that has always rankled older people.

专家称老人语言,就是那种连哄带骗、带有轻蔑的用语,常常惹火年长的人。

2 But when I hear it, it raises my hackles.

但是我听了这，就一肚子火。

3 Now studies are finding that the insults can have health consequences, especially if people mutely accept the attitudes behind them.

现在的研究表明，这种"侮辱性"的称呼有害健康，尤其是当人们以默然的态度接受时。

4 If addressed as infants, some showed their irritation by grimacing, screaming or refusing to do what staff members asked of them.

如果像对婴儿一样对他们说话，他们更会借由扮鬼脸、尖叫或拒绝合作来发泄他们的愤怒。

5 "It's harder to change," Dr. Levy said, "because people spend so much of their lives observing it without having a stake in it, not realizing it's belittling to call someone that."

"这很难改变，"利维教授说，"因为在人的一生中经常会说起这些词，而没有考虑到这些词与老年人之间的利害关系，人们没有意识到这样称呼人是对人的蔑视。"

· 讨论 ·

1 What's your opinion about "elderspeak"?

2 How did the patients react when nurses addressed to them as infants?

3 Why Ms. Plummer wrote "I exploded" in the New York Times blog?

• Extensive Reading •

Animal restaurant in Los Angeles

By S. Irene Virbila, Times Restaurant Critic

August 20, 2008

Entertainment Column of Los Angeles Times

TWO "food dudes" — laid-back, long-haired cooks who grew up in Florida and are culinary graduates of the Art Institute of Fort Lauderdale — make their way to California and end up at the late Chadwick in Beverly Hills working with Ben Ford and Govind Armstrong. In 2004, the dudes, Jon Shook and Vinny Dotolo, found Caramelized Productions, a catering company. Soon, they're starring in the Food Network docudrama series, "Two Dudes Catering," which purports to show "two young renegade chefs who play by their own rules" in "the big time world of Hollywood catering."

This spring they opened Animal, a restaurant on Fairfax Avenue that picks up on the idea of Fergus Henderson's London restaurant St. John and focuses on rustic meat-centric cooking. Their book "Two Dudes, One Pan: Maximum Flavor From a Minimalist Kitchen" is due out Aug. 26.

I want to root for these two out-of-towners who have managed to open their own restaurant. I applaud Animal's concept and aesthetic — dietarily incorrect, exuberant and indulgent, with bacon popping up in almost every dish. But while some of the dishes are pretty good, I'm finding it hard to fall for this restaurant, despite the enthusiastic young hipsters all around the dining room shouting out that the grits are amazing and the ribs fabulous.

With heavy wood tabletops that look smoked or scorched, a plywood banquette lining one wall and old-fashioned bare filament light bulbs screwed into porcelain fixtures on the walls, Animal cultivates that minimalist, bare-bones look. There's a bar at the back where you can hang, waiting for a table, and a patio of sorts up front where smokers take a break.

Sweet and salty

THE MENU, printed on brown recycled paper in a faint italic hand, is hard to read. Nevermind, it hardly changes from week to week, which tells me the two young chefs have a fairly small repertoire. Their cooking is on the rough side of rustic and tends to be greasy, but made with good ingredients. Dishes can go well over the top with too many flavors competing for attention and wallowing in too much sauce.

I know the chefs are having a ball in the kitchen, dreaming up dishes, sending plates out to friends and fans — but somebody has to get a grip. Hide the salt and the sugar (too much of either or both escape onto the plates) and maybe — just a thought — cut back on the bacon.

OK, one rich, gooey dish is fun. And that would be the hot and bubbling plate of petite Basque cheese melted over Fra' Mani chorizo with stiff toasts of garlic bread to scoop up the molten mass. This is great, especially with a glass of beer. If you're a crowd, you might like to pair it with an order of fried hominy with lime squeezed over to cut the salt.

The ribs — cooked 10 hours, the affable waiter tells us, in a balsamic glaze — are good too, falling-off-the-bones tender. If, however, you like to sink your teeth into your ribs, these are not for you. I like that they serve them with a bread salad with heirloom tomatoes. All in all, though, after eating here, I find myself longing for vegetables.

The closest you can get are the khaki-colored, long-cooked Romano beans dressed in lemon and chili flakes and covered with pecorino shavings — and some pancetta. These, I have to say, are wonderful but don't really satisfy that craving for something green.

Or you can get braised marinated leeks with spinach, poached egg and bacon, but the result is a gooey mess of flavors, everything soft and indistinct. The dudes' territory is strictly comfort zone.

Shaved asparagus is a more focused dish, drizzled with a bacon vinaigrette and topped with a poached egg and Grana Padano cheese. Diced raw amberjack tossed with sliced nectarines and orange segments in a dressing lighted up with serrano chiles is terrific, an oddball mix of flavors that really zaps those taste buds.

A first course of foie gras with biscuit and gravy, a honey-laced biscuit topped with a small piece of excellent seared foie gras, the whole thing sitting in a gratin dish with enough sweet gravy to fuel the entire room, is puzzling. I see the point: Most chefs pair something sweet with foie gras. But it also needs some acidity to cut the sweetness. For me, this is too cloying to live.

I'm just as puzzled by the idea of serving the huge Tomahawk rib-eye steak for two in foie gras sauce in the middle of summer. Piling on the richness and the tony ingredients doesn't always result in something amazing. And the menu offers little relief from the sweetness and richness. What's needed are some perspective and discipline.

Fried quail — tender, bursting with juice in a shaggy golden crust — is a charming idea. But it's served on top of Anson Mills grits that taste as if they've been cooked in heavy cream. Unfortunately, the long-cooked greens that accompany them are so salty, they're inedible. To add to the salt quotient on the plate, there's more slab bacon on the side.

Order pork chops and you get two big ones, salty enough that I seriously wonder if someone left them in the brine too long. Too bad, it's a waste of beautiful pork. Niman Ranch flatiron steak is fussed up with Madeira, chanterelles, potatoes and sweetbreads one time, another version substitutes a bordelaise sauce for the Madeira, and creamed leeks and corn for the chanterelles and potatoes. In the end, you may want to shout out, let my steak be! Please.

A taste for beer

AT ANIMAL, only hearty appetites need apply, preferably ones that can also accommodate a big, cold glass of beer rather than wine with dinner, because the wine list is pretty basic. It encompasses about 20 selections and all of them can be had by the glass, carafe or bottle. A bottle is always a better buy, especially here, when most are well under $50.

Oddly enough, it lists more whites than reds, which could be an advantage since Animal's chefs do better with fish than with meat. Grilled branzino arrives whole and is deftly filleted at the table. If only they'd cut down a little on the amount of brown butter and capers, the branzino would be one of the best in town (it might help the bottom line too, because it looks as if somebody dropped an entire jar of capers over my fish).

Slow down, calm down, I want to say. The dudes can cook and cook well if the delicious, firm turbot in fresh tomato sauce with marrow beans and favas is any example.

Desserts are appealing, but not very adventurous. Especially the fruit crisps, which vary with what's around. One night it could be strawberry rhubarb; another nectarine and blueberries, with a fused topping that's more like a cookie than a crisp or crumble — and tastes like one too. As for the dudes' signature bacon chocolate crunch bar? I like it. The bacon stands in for a light sprinkling of salt, and it works.

第 11 章

UNIT 11

WORLD ENVIRONMENT

• Text •

背景参考

随着全球气候的变暖以及其带来的一系列危害，人们正努力采取措施来抑制这种趋势的发展。1992 年联合国专门制订了《联合国气候变化框架公约》，该公约于同年在巴西里约热内卢签署生效。依据该公约，发达国家同意在 2000 年之前将他们释放到大气层的二氧化碳及其他“温室气体”的排放量降至 1990 年时的水平。另外，这些每年的二氧化碳合计排放量占到全球二氧化碳总排放量 60% 的国家还同意将相关技术和信息转让给发展中国家。发展中国家能通过发达国家转让来的技术，应对环境变化带来的挑战。截至 2004 年 5 月，已有 189 个国家正式批准了上述公约。

但气候变暖带来的危害程度却不容乐观，北极地区的变暖速度正逐渐加快，不采取有效手段遏制这种趋势的话，在不久的将来，北极地区的冰层将离我们远去。

根据科学家的研究，在 2060 年至 2100 年间，夏季北冰洋的海冰可能会完全消失。这一研究报告是 250 名科学家受北极周边包括美国、加拿大、俄罗斯、丹麦、挪威、瑞典、芬兰和冰岛在内的 8 个国家政府的委托，历经 4 年完成的，可以说是科学家迄今对地球某一地区气候变化趋势进行的最深入的研究。

科学家们在研究中发现，北冰洋海冰的厚度和面积都已急剧缩小。根据潜艇采集的数据，从20世纪60年代至90年代，这一地区冰山的水下部分已萎缩了约40%。尽管近年来由于北冰洋的洋流出现变化，暖流减少，使浮冰融化速度有所减慢，但科学家们仍认为，北冰洋"夏季无冰"的趋势依然会发展[1]。

然而，北冰洋夏季海冰的消失反而引起了一些利益集团的极大兴趣。随着全球变暖现象的加剧，北冰洋可能将成为一座新的能源宝库，北冰洋上诸如汉斯岛等岛屿的战略重要性也大大提高。目前，加拿大和丹麦对汉斯岛的主权争夺已进入了白热化[2]状态。随着气温不断上升，北冰洋水域面积不断扩大，进而增加了通航能力。两个军事强国，美国与英国也开始对北冰洋水域虎视眈眈，代号为"2007·冰"军演不只是为了探索巴拿马运河之外大西洋到太平洋的潜艇部队调动通道，也是为了争夺北极地区还未开采的自然资源。

据广州日报报道，美国海岸警卫队向阿拉斯加州北部海岸派出一个小组，为在当地修建基地做准备。美联社也报道，基地将加强海岸警卫队监控北极地区的能力。北冰洋冰层融化加速，北极地区航运、自然资源价值凸现，周边国家竞争激烈。地球资源不断匮乏，一些发达国家随即将视线转移到这些尚未开采过的地区，南北两极就自然成为了他们的牺牲品。两极地区拥有的丰富的自然资源，随着海冰的逐渐消失，使开采两极地区有了现实的可能性。

随着北冰洋冰层融化持续加速，北极地区巨大航运潜力愈发凸显，势必造成北极地区大规模的人类活动，一些利益集团不应只关注其美好的开发前景，而更应关注大规模人类活动给北极地区所带来的正反两方面的影响。

参考文献

[1] 世界新闻报. 北冰洋将成"无冰洋"？http://gb.cri.cn,2004-11-09.
[2] 关注全球变暖的正面效应. http://guancha.gmw.cn,2007-03-26.

New Coast Guard Task in Arctic's Warming Seas

By MATTHEW L. WALD and ANDREW C. REVKIN

Published: *October* 19, 2007
U.S. Column of the New York Times

WASHINGTON — For most of human history, the Arctic Ocean has been an ice-locked frontier[1]. **But now, in one of the most concrete signs of the effect of a warming climate on government operations, the Coast Guard is planning its first operating base there as a way of dealing with the cruise ships and the tankers that are already beginning to ply Arctic waters.**

With increasingly long seasons of open water in the region, the Coast Guard has also begun discussions with the Russians about controlling anticipated ship traffic through the Bering Strait, which until now has been crossed mainly by ice-breaking research vessels and native seal and walrus hunters.

The Coast Guard says its base, which would probably be near the United States' northernmost town, Barrow, Alaska, on the North Slope coast, would be seasonal and would initially have just a helicopter equipped for cold-weather operations and several small boats.

But given continued warming, that small base, which could be in place by next spring, would be expanded later to help speed responses to oil spills from tankers that the Coast Guard believes could eventually carry shipments from Scandinavia to Asia through the Bering Strait. Such a long-hoped-for polar route would cut 5,000 miles or more from a journey that would otherwise entail passage through the Panama Canal or the Suez[2].

The Coast Guard is also concerned about being able to respond to emergencies involving cruise ships, which are already starting to operate in summers in parts of the Arctic Ocean.

And in yet a further kind of new activity abetted by warming seas, Royal Dutch Shell is preparing for exploratory oil drilling off Alaska's Arctic coast beginning next year.

"I'm not sure I'm qualified to talk about the scientific issues related to global warming," the Coast Guard commandant, Adm. Thad W. Allen, said in an interview. "All we know is we have an operating environment we're responsible for, and it's changing."

The commander of the Coast Guard's Alaska district, Rear Adm. Arthur E. Brooks, said in a telephone interview that the expansion of open water as summer sea ice pulls back means that "almost everything the U. S. does will be doable in the Arctic, we think[3]."

A new survey by American oceanographers of the seafloor north of Alaska, completed last month aboard the Coast Guard icebreaker Healy, provides fresh evidence that the United States has much at stake[4] in the region. The sonar studies found hints that thousands of square miles of additional seafloor could potentially be under American control. That floor might yield important deposits of oil, gas or minerals in coming decades, government studies have concluded.

So far did the sea ice pull back this summer that the expedition was able to scan the bottom several hundred miles farther north than in previous surveys, said the project's director, Larry Mayer, an oceanographer at the University of New Hampshire. The team found long sloping extensions 200 miles beyond previous estimates[5].

Though more surveys will be needed to firm up any American claim, countries have a right to expand their control of seabed resources well beyond the continental shelves bordering their coasts if they can find such sloping extensions[6]. That right is guaranteed by the United Nations Law of the Sea treaty, which, after years of fights in Congress, the United States appears poised to ratify. The treaty has the support of President Bush, but ratification requires approval by two-thirds of the Senate.

Senior State Department officials say the United States has to become more involved in the region, and are urging other countries to cooperate to encourage international trade through the Far North.

"Having a safe, secure and reliable Arctic shipping regime is vital to the proper development of Arctic resources, especially now given the extent of Arctic ice retreat we witnessed this past summer[7]," Assistant Secretary of State Daniel S. Sullivan said Monday at an international conference in Anchorage[8]. "We can have such a regime only through cooperation, not competition, among Arctic nations. Denial of passage through international waterways, even though they may be territorial waters, and burdensome transit requirements will not benefit any nation in the long run."

The change in Arctic sea and ice conditions has indeed been remarkable, as one stark example demonstrates. **The Coast Guard recently produced a video commemorating the transit of the Northwest Passage in the summer of 1957 by three**

cutters that became icebound, forcing the crews to dynamite the ice to free themselves. Now open water is the norm in summers along many Arctic coasts.

The resulting increase in Arctic activity will mean a greater need for search and rescue capabilities and for environmental protection, Coast Guard officials say. In fact, Admiral Allen says ship traffic could turn the Bering Strait into a choke point[9] like the Strait of Gibraltar.

Environmentalists view the Coast Guard's interest with dismay about what it suggests for the future of a fragile environment, but also with some relief.

"We should be taking a hard look as a nation at what do we need to do to adequately protect the environment, faced with that kind of massive change in risk," said Pamela A. Miller, the Arctic coordinator at the Northern Alaska Environmental Center, in Fairbanks.

Mead Treadwell, an Anchorage businessman who is chairman of the Arctic Research Commission, created by Congress to advise the government on scientific and other issues in the region, said the Coast Guard's new plans were only fair[10].

"It is high time that our coastline in the north enjoyed the same protections other states' coastal residents have from the Coast Guard," he said[11]. "The Arctic may be warming, but there's no indication that conditions at sea are getting any safer."

Matthew L. Wald reported from Washington, and Andrew C. Revkin from New York.

难点注释

1 ice-locked frontier 海冰覆盖的边境

2 Such a long-hoped-for polar route would cut 5,000 miles or more from a journey that would otherwise entail passage through the Panama Canal or the Suez.

这个心系已久的极地路线将缩减5000英里或者更多的航行里程，不然的话，必须取道巴拿马或者苏伊士运河航行。

3 The commander of the Coast Guard's Alaska district, Rear Adm. Arthur E. Brooks, said in a telephone interview that the expansion of open water as

summer sea ice pulls back means that "almost everything the U.S. does will be doable in the Arctic, we think."

海岸警卫队阿拉斯加区长官，海军上将 Arthur E. Brooks 在电话采访中说到，"我们认为，夏季海冰消失导致日益扩大的水域使得美国在别的地方开展的活动在北极也有了可能。"

4 at stake 处于危险中

5 The team found long sloping extensions 200 miles beyond previous estimates.

考察队通过先前估计，发现一块长斜坡向北延伸 200 英里。

6 Though more surveys will be needed to firm up any American claim, countries have a right to expand their control of seabed resources well beyond the continental shelves bordering their coasts if they can find such sloping extensions.

尽管还需要更多的实地考察才能强化美国的领土主张，但是一些国家只要能找到这样的斜坡延展区，就可以对环绕海岸线的大陆架之外的海底资源拥有更多的支配权。

7 especially now given the extent of Arctic ice retreat we witnessed this past summer.

尤其考虑到今夏，我们在北极目睹了极地冰缩开辟了大片水域的情形下。

8 Anchorage 安克拉治

美国阿拉斯加州最大城市，人口数为 279,671(2007 年)。

It is a consolidated city-borough in the U.S. state of Alaska, with an estimated 279,671 municipal residents in 2007. (*From Wikipedia, the free encyclopedia*)

9 choke point 瓶颈

10 the Coast Guard's new plans were only fair

海岸警卫队的新计划只看到了美好的一面。

11 "It is high time that our coastline in the north enjoyed the same protections other states' coastal residents have from the Coast Guard," he said.

他说，"跟其他海岸居民一样，现在正是海岸警卫队为北部海域提供环境保护的好时候"。

精华长句

1 But now, in one of the most concrete signs of the effect of a warming climate on government operations, the Coast Guard is planning its first operating base there as a way of dealing with the cruise ships and the tankers that are already beginning to ply Arctic waters.

但如今，气候变暖对政府运作的影响所体现的真实迹象之一就是海岸警卫队计划在北冰洋建立它的第一个工作基地，此基地能安置往返于北极水域巡洋舰以及油轮。

2 With increasingly long seasons of open water in the region, the Coast Guard has also begun discussions with the Russians about controlling anticipated ship traffic through the Bering Strait, which until now has been crossed mainly by ice-breaking research vessels and native seal and walrus hunters.

随着北冰洋区域无冰水面持续时间越来越长，海岸警卫队已经开始与俄罗斯方面展开讨论，目的在于控制白令海峡的过往船只量，直到现在，白令海峡上运行的主要是破冰科考船以及海豹和海象捕猎者船只。

3 But given continued warming, that small base, which could be in place by next spring, would be expanded later to help speed responses to oil spills from tankers that the Coast Guard believes could eventually carry shipments from Scandinavia to Asia through the Bering Strait.

但是考虑到气候持续变暖，海岸警卫队小型基地将在明年春天启用，这个基地能对油轮漏油做出快速反应，与此同时，海岸警卫队认为，装满石油的油轮可从斯堪的纳维亚半岛穿过白令海峡直抵亚洲。

4 The Coast Guard recently produced a video commemorating the transit of the Northwest Passage in the summer of 1957 by three cutters that became icebound, forcing the crews to dynamite the ice to free themselves.

海岸警卫队展示了一段录像，录像纪念的是 1957 年夏季船员们通过西北水道的过程：三台切割机被冰封在海里，船员们不得不用炸药使自己脱身。

5 "We should be taking a hard look as a nation at what do we need to do to adequately protect the environment, faced with that kind of massive change in risk," said Pamela A. Miller, the Arctic coordinator at the Northern Alaska Environmental Center, in Fairbanks.

在费尔班克斯的北阿拉斯加环境中心工作的极地协调员 Pamela A. Miller 说到:"面对人类活动大规模增多所可能带来的危险,一个国家应认真审视我们采取哪些行动充分保护这一地区的环境。"

讨论

1 How do you comment on the effect of Global Warming?

2 What are the most unusual weather conditions you have ever experienced?

3 What do we need to do to adequately protect the environment?

• Extensive Reading •

The Top 20 Effects of Global warming

September 24, 2007

This piece is from the Center for American Progress Action Fund's Mic Check Radio. Energy & Environment column in Center for American Progress

Global Warming Wrecks All the Fun

Say Goodbye to French Wines

Wacky temperatures and rain cycles brought on by global warming are threatening something very important: Wine. Scientists believe global warming will "shift viticultural regions toward the poles, cooler coastal zones and higher elevations." What that means in regular language: Get ready to say bye-bye to French Bordeaux and hello to British champagne. [LA Times]

Say Goodbye to Light and Dry Wines

Warmer temperatures mean grapes in California and France develop their sugars too quickly, well before their other flavors. As a result, growers are forced to either a) leave the grapes on the vines longer, which dramatically raises the alcoholic content of the fruit or b) pick the grapes too soon and make overly sweet wine that tastes like jam. [Washington Post]

Say Goodbye to Pinot Noir

The reason you adore pinot noir is that it comes from a notoriously temperamental thin-skinned grape that thrives in cool climates. Warmer temperatures are already damaging the pinots from Oregon, "baking away" the grape's berry flavors. [Bloomberg]

Say Goodbye to Baseball

The future of the ash tree—from which all baseball bats are made—is in danger of disappearing, thanks to a combination of killer beetles and global warming. [NY Times]

Say Goodbye to Christmas Trees

The Pine Bark Beetle, which feeds on and kills pine trees, used to be held in control by cold winter temperatures. Now the species is thriving and killing off entire forests in British Columbia, unchecked. [Seattle Post Intelligencer]

Say Goodbye to the Beautiful Alaska Vacation

Warmer weather allowed Spruce Bark Beetles to live longer, hardier lives in the forests of Kenai Peninsula in Alaska, where they killed off a section of spruce forest the size of Connecticut. [Alaska Science Forum]

Say Goodbye to Fly Fishing

As water temperatures continue to rise, researchers say rainbow trout, "already at the southern limits" of their temperature ranges in the Appalachian mountains, could disappear there over the next century. [Softpedia]

Say Goodbye to Ski Competitions

Unusually warmer winters caused the International Ski Federation to cancel last year's Alpine skiing World Cup and opening races in Soelden, Austria. Skiers are also hard-pressed now to find places for year-round training. Olympic gold medalist Anja Paerson: "Of course we're all very worried about the future of our sport. Every year we have more trouble finding places to train." [NY Times]

Say Goodbye to Ski Vacations

Slopes on the East Coast last year closed months ahead of time due to warmer weather, some losing as much as a third of their season. [Washington Post]

Say Hello to Really Tacky Fake Ski Vacations

Weiner Air Force and former House Majority Leader Dick Armey are building a year-round ski resort in Texas, with "wet, white Astroturf with bristles" standing in for snow to make up for all the closed resorts around the country. [WSJ]

Say Goodbye to That Snorkeling Vacation

The elkhorn coral which used to line the floor of the Caribbean are nearly gone, "victims of pollution, warmer water and acidification from the greenhouse gas carbon dioxide seeping into oceans." [Denver Post]

Say Goodbye to That Tropical Island Vacation

Indonesia's environment minister announced this year that scientific studies estimate about 2,000 of the country's lush tropical islands could disappear by 2030 due to rising sea levels. [ABC News]

Say Goodbye to Cool Cultural Landmarks

The World Monuments Fund recently added "global warming" as a threat in their list of the top 100 threatened cultural landmarks. "On Herschel Island, Canada, melting permafrost threatens ancient Inuit sites and a historic whaling town. In Chinguetti, Mauritania, the desert is encroaching on an ancient mosque. In Antarctica, a hut once used by British explorer Captain Robert Falcon Scott has survived almost a century of freezing conditions but is now in danger of being engulfed by increasingly heavy snows." [AP]

Say Goodbye to Salmon Dinners

Get ready for a lot more chicken dinners: Wild pacific salmon have already vanished from 40 percent of their traditional habitats in the Northwest and the NRDC warns warmer temperatures are going to erase 41 percent of their habitat by 2090. [ENS]

Say Goodbye to Lobster Dinners

Lobsters thrive in the chilly waters of New England, but recent numbers show that as those waters have warmed up, "the big-clawed American lobster—prized for its delicate, sweet flesh—has been withering at an alarming rate from New York state to Massachusetts." [AP]

Say Goodbye to Discoveries of Sharks That Can Walk

Scientists recently revealed a "lost world" of marine life off the coast of Indonesia, including 20 new species of corals, 8 species of shrimp, a technicolor fish that "flashes" bright pink, yellow, blue, and green hues, and sharks that "walk" on their fins. ("Avon Lady. Candygram.") However, marine biologists warn the threats posed by global warming means millions of other crazy cool sea creatures may become extinct before we ever discover them. [ABC]

Say Goodbye to Meadows of Wildflowers

Scientists think global warming could wipe out a fifth of the wildflower species in the western United States. They'll be replaced by dominant grasses. [National Wildlife Federation]

Say Goodbye to Guacamole

Scientists from the Lawrence Livermore National Laboratory predict hotter temps will cause a 40 percent drop in California's avocado production over the next 40 years. [Lawrence Livermore National Lab]

Say Goodbye to Mixed Nuts

Guess you'll have to start eating pretzels at the bar instead: Scientists from the Lawrence Livermore National Laboratory predict hotter temps will cause a 20 percent drop in California's almond and walnut crops over the next 40 years. [Science Daily]

Say Goodbye to French Fries

Scientists from the Consultative Group on International Agricultural Research say warmer temperatures are killing off wild relatives of potato and peanut plants, "threatening a valuable source of genes necessary to help these food crops fight pests and drought." [AP]

第 12 章
UNIT 12
HEALTH

• Text •

背景参考

经济危机与健康

一场经济危机袭来，让股市崩盘，让各大公司裁员，让货币贬值，让整个社会的经济环境都进入了不健康的状态。与此同时，不健康的经济环境还会对你的身心健康产生一系列直接的影响。

世界卫生组织不久前曾经发出警告，全球经济危机可能导致精神健康问题加剧。经济危机的到来，让整个世界的经济陷入低谷，人们开始抛售股票，人们疯狂加班工作，人们的生活水平下降，社会压力、职场压力、生活压力骤增。这些压力压得人们喘不过气来，自杀现象也随之增多。今年年初，德国亿万富翁阿道夫・默克勒卧轨自杀[1]，美国亿万富翁史蒂文・古德开枪自杀[2]，这些例子都可以从一定程度上反映经济危机对个人心理健康的危害，因此保持平衡的心境对于战胜经济危机显得十分之必要。

经济危机不仅影响着个人的心理健康，还严重影响着个人的身体健康。据俄罗斯《新消息报》报道，经济危机让所有俄罗斯人勒紧腰带过日子，除了削减旅游度假支出，放弃购买新车等奢侈品外，很多家庭还不得不在吃饭问题上做文章，尽量减少最基本的生活开支。专家们警告这不会有任何好结果，因为食用质低价廉的食品，甚至放弃某些种类的食品，很可能打破人体内的营养平衡，并由此导致一系列严重的健康问题。列瓦达民调中心居民收入与消费研究部门的研究人员娜塔利娅・邦达连科告诉记者，她们一家人不久前也开始"节食"。她说："我们家有四口人——我、丈夫和两个儿子。我在生小儿子前离职，家里只靠丈夫一个人养活，当时的情况并不是很坏。但自丈夫今年 4 月失业后，我们就不得不大幅节省开支，包括减少食品花销。最近一个月里，我们的餐桌上既没有肉，也没有甜食和小点心，有时甚至连蔬菜、水果也不敢买了。我们现在只能希望情况尽快改变，丈夫能重新找到稳定的工作。"[3]

经济危机带给你的健康只是破坏吗?答案是否定的。

在危机中，一部分人工作强度下降了，压力减少了，身体也健康多了。在经济发展时期，有些人要经常加班加点工作，熬夜到凌晨，心脏一直处于超负荷状态。危机来了，企业订单少了，白天也不忙了，人们可以按时下班了，心脏也恢复活力了。更为重要的是，危机到来，人们应酬少了，有更多时间可以做户外运动，增强身体体质。

另一方面，经济危机中，时间的价值相对下降，人们会抽出更多时间和家人相处，有利于和谐家庭的建立。在以前经济高速发展时期，父母都会各自为了挣更多的钱而争分夺秒地工作，往往忽略孩子和家庭；但现在有些父母下岗，有些父母工作强度下降，他们会倾向把剩余时间留给家庭，这对孩子的健康成长以及家庭的和谐发展都有很大好处。

经济危机对个人健康的影响，我们不能一概而论，对不同的人可能产生不同的影响，但无论影响如何，我们都应该想办法身心健康地度过经济危机，迎接阳光灿烂的明天。

参考文献

[1] 德第五大亿万富翁默克勒卧轨自杀身亡. http://www.jfdaily.com, 2009-01-07.

[2] 亿万富翁史蒂文·古德自杀 多名欧美富翁走不归路. http://news.csonline.com, 2009-01-07.

[3] 俄罗斯居民节食渡经济危机 面临严重健康问题. http://www.china.com.cn, 2009-05-13.

Are Bad Times Healthy?

By TARA PARKER-POPE

Published: *October* 7, 2008

Science Column of The New York Times

Most people are worried about the health of the economy. But does the economy also affect your health?

It does, but not always in ways you might expect. The data on how an economic downturn influences an individual's health are surprisingly mixed.

It's clear that long-term economic gains lead to improvements in a population's overall health, in developing and industrialized societies alike.

But whether the current economic slump[1] will take a toll on your own health depends, in part, on your health habits when times are good. And economic studies suggest that people tend not to take care of themselves in boom times — drinking too much (especially before driving), dining on fat-laden restaurant meals and skipping exercise and doctors' appointments because of work-related time commitments.

"The value of time is higher during good economic times," said Grant Miller, an assistant professor of medicine at Stanford. **"So people work more and do less of the things that are good for them, like cooking at home and exercising** and people experience more stress due to the rigors[2] of hard work during booms."

Similar patterns have been seen in some developing nations. Dr. Miller, who is studying the effects of fluctuating[3] coffee prices on health in Colombia, says that even though falling prices are bad for the economy, they appear to improve health and mortality rates. When prices are low, laborers have more time to care for their children.

"When coffee prices suddenly rise, people work harder on their coffee plots and spend less time doing things around the home, including things that are good for their children," he said. "Because the things that matter most for infant and child health in rural Colombia aren't expensive, but require a substantial[4] amount of time — such as breast-feeding, bringing clean water from far away, taking your child to a distant health clinic for free vaccinations — infant and child mortality rates rise."

In this country, a similar effect appeared in the Dust Bowl during the Great Depression, according to a 2007 paper by Dr. Miller and colleagues in The Proceedings of the National Academy of Sciences.

The data seem to contradict[5] research in the 1970s suggesting that in hard times there are more deaths from heart disease, cirrhosis, suicide and homicide, as well as more admissions to mental hospitals. But those findings have not been replicated, and several economists have pointed out flaws in the research.

In May 2000, the Quarterly Journal of Economics published a surprising paper called "Are Recessions Good for Your Health?" by Christopher J. Ruhm, professor of economics at the University of North Carolina, Greensboro, based on an analysis measuring death rates and health behavior against economic shifts and jobless rates from 1972 to 1991.

Dr. Ruhm found that death rates declined sharply in the 1974 and 1982 recessions, and increased in the economic recovery of the 1980s. An increase of one percentage point in state unemployment rates correlated with a 0.5 percentage point decline in the death rate — or about 5 fewer deaths per 100,000 people. Over all, the death rate fell by more than 8 percent in the 20-year period of mostly economic decline, led by drops in heart disease and car crashes.

The economic downturn did appear to take a toll on factors having less to do with prevention and more to do with mental well-being and access to health care. For instance, cancer deaths rose 23 percent, and deaths from flu and pneumonia increased slightly. Suicides rose 2 percent, homicides 12 percent.

The issue that may matter most in an economic crisis is not related to jobs or income, but whether the slump widens the gap between rich and poor, and whether there is an adequate health safety net available to those who have lost their jobs and insurance.

During a decade of economic recession[6] in Japan that began in the 1990s, people who were unemployed were twice as likely to be in poor health than those with secure jobs. During Peru's severe economic crisis in the 1980s, infant mortality jumped 2.5 percentage points — about 17,000 more children who died as public health spending and social programs collapsed.

In August, researchers from the Free University of Amsterdam looked at health studies of twins in Denmark. They found that individuals born in a recession were at higher risk for heart problems later in life and lived, on average, 15 months less than those born under better conditions.

Gerard J. van den Berg, an economics professor who was a co-author of the study, said babies in poor households suffered the most in a recession, because their families lacked access to[7] good health care. Poor economic conditions can also cause stress that may interfere with[8] parent bonding and childhood development, he said.

He noted that other studies had found that recessions can benefit babies by giving their parents more time at home.

"This scenario may be relevant for well-to-do families where one of the parents loses a job and the other still brings in enough money," he said. "But in a crisis where the family may have to incur huge housing-cost losses and the household income is insufficient for adequate[9] nutrition and health care, the adverse effects of being born in a recession seem much more relevant."

In this country, there are already signs of the economy's effect on health. In May, the market research firm Information Resources reported that 53 percent of consumers said they were cooking from scratch[10] more than they did just six months before — in part, no doubt, because of the rising cost of prepared foods. At the same time, health insurance costs are rising. With premiums[11] and co-payments, the average employee with insurance pays nearly one-third of medical costs — about twice as much as four years ago, according to Paul H. Keckley, executive director of the Deloitte Center for Health Solutions.

In the United States, which unlike other industrialized nations lacks a national health plan, the looming recession may take a greater toll. About 46 million Americans lack health insurance, Dr. Keckley says, and even among the 179 million who have it, an estimated 1 in 7 would be bankrupted by a single health crisis.

The economic downturn "is not good news for the health care industry," he said. "There may be slivers[12] of positive, but I view this as sobering."

难点注释

1 slump 暴跌，不景气，下降，消沉，萎靡

2 rigor 严格，苛刻，艰苦

3 fluctuate 变动，动摇，使动摇，使波动

4 substantial 实质上的,有内容的,物质的

5 contradict 否定,反驳

6 recession 后退,不景气

7 access to 接近,有权使用

8 interfere with 打扰

9 adequate 足够的,能满足需要的,胜任的,适当的

10 scratch 抓痕,刮擦声,乱涂

11 premium 奖品,额外补贴,津贴,奖金

12 sliver 裂片,梳毛,薄片

精华长句

1 But whether the current economic slump will take a toll on your own health depends, in part, on your health habits when times are good.
但是,目前的经济下滑是否会对你自身的健康造成影响,一大部分取决于当经济环境好时你的生活习惯。

2 So people work more and do less of the things that are good for them, like cooking at home and exercising.
因此人们用更多的时间工作,用更少的时间做对自身有益的事情,比如在家烹饪和运动。

3 The economic downturn did appear to take a toll on factors having less to do with prevention and more to do with mental well-being and access to health care.
经济的下滑确实会对某些因素产生破坏,而这些因素与预防的关系较小,与精神快乐和医疗保健关系密切。

4 During a decade of economic recession in Japan that began in the 1990s, people who were unemployed were twice as likely to be in poor health than those with secure jobs.
日本的经济下滑开始于90年代并持续了十多年,在这期间,失业人群的健康水平比拥有安定职业的人群健康水平相差近两倍左右。

5 In the United States, which unlike other industrialized nations lacks a national health plan, the looming recession may take a greater toll.

与其他工业化国家不同，美国缺乏国家医疗保险计划，即将到来的衰退可能造成更大的损失。

讨论

1 "The value of time is higher during good economic times." Do you agree or disagree? Why?

2 How do you think of the relationship between the economic crisis and people's health?

3 Could you give some suggestion about how to be healthy during bad economic times?

• Extensive Reading •

Fan in Room Seems to Cut Infants' Risk of Crib Death

By TARA PARKER-POPE

Published: *October* 6, 2008

Health Column of The New York Times

Sleeping in a room with a fan lowers a baby's risk of sudden infant death syndrome by 72 percent, a new study has found.

The finding, published Monday in The Archives of Pediatrics and Adolescent Medicine, is the latest evidence to suggest that a baby's sleep environment is a critical factor in the risk of SIDS, which is diagnosed when an infant's sudden death cannot be explained by other factors.

The study was not designed to identify why fans make a difference, but researchers said they thought that by circulating air, fans lowered the risk of "rebreathing" exhaled carbon dioxide. That risk has been suggested as a reason the rate of SIDS is higher when children sleep on their stomach, in a soft bed or without a pacifier.

Since 1992 the rate of SIDS deaths has dropped by more than half, to about one death per 2,000 live births from 2.4 per 1,000. The decline is linked to a national "Back to Sleep" campaign that promotes putting babies on their back instead of their stomach, which has been shown to lower the risk of sudden death.

The American Academy of Pediatrics also recommends that parents avoid soft bedding, allow babies to use a pacifier and avoid overheating a baby's room.

Despite the gains, SIDS continues to be the leading cause of death in babies under the age of 1, and researchers are looking for more measures to lower the risk.

The latest study compared 185 babies who had died of SIDS with 312 randomly selected babies and matched them by age, race, ethnic group and country of origin.

"Even though we don't know why certain babies are more susceptible, sleeping environment matters," said a co-author of the study, Dr. De-Kun Li, a reproductive and perinatal epidemiologist at Kaiser Permanente's division of research in Oakland, Calif.

Parents who worry that their child will be chilled by a fan should know that fans do not cool the air; they just move air around. A baby will feel a chill only if he or she is perspiring, doctors say.

Parents who use fans in a child's room should make sure to take normal safety precautions, keeping cords out of the way and making sure the fan cannot be knocked down by a toddler or pet.

Dr. Li said the use of fans should not replace other sleeping strategies for lowering SIDS, like removing soft bedding and putting babies on their back. He noted that the gains shown in the study were an average for the whole group, including for babies whose care did not meet the guidelines. Still, even if a baby had a safe sleeping environment, the risk of SIDS was lowered by about 16 percent for those who had a fan in the room, although the trend was not statistically significant.

"If parents wanted to do more to reduce the baby's SIDS risk," he said, "they can add a fan."

第 13 章

UNIT 13

LANGUAGE FEATURES

1 英文报刊的内容特点

英文报刊在内容上具有以下几个突出的特点：

首先，内容通俗新颖，真实性强，关注时事热点，紧跟时代步伐，追踪流行因素。报刊阅读的一大优势在于内容真实、鲜活、富有感染力。报刊文章是社会真实事件的反映，由于此类文章贴近生活实际，与时俱进，读者对社会的了解可以直接来自于英文报刊。报刊中报道的大都是国内外刚刚发生的重要事件，描述的人物也多是最近的新闻人物或极具人气的文体明星，为读者提供了许多最近、最新的热门话题。阅读这些文章有助于读者了解时事，了解现实生活。

其次，信息量大，内容丰富，话题涉猎广泛、新颖，而且语言表达地道、生动，能够给读者提供较大的选择空间，从内容不同的文章中可以获取文化、政治、经济、科技等各个领域的信息。报刊中有国内外一周要闻和时事论坛，有热点讨论、校园生活、美文赏析，还有影视娱乐、时尚和体育新闻等等，其内容丰富多彩，读者不仅能够拓宽知识面，而且还能接触新鲜的词汇和地道的语言表达。

第三，趣味性强。英文报刊丰富多彩的内容和精美的图片能够强烈地吸引读者，提高阅读兴趣。

第四，词语实用。从某种意义上讲，报刊英语就是当代英语，以较快的速度反映英语的发展和变化。语言在使用过程中总是发生着日新月异的变化，这些变化都迅速体现在英文报刊中，有助于读者把握语言动态。如科技与医学领域的词汇，一般先出现在报刊新闻中，后才逐渐被人们所认识，如 SARS，bird flu，blog 等。从英语用词讲，词汇的使用频率在实际生活中是不一样的，某一些词汇在某一新闻特定时期会重复出现，如 terrorist attack，nuclear weapon 等。

2 英文报刊标题的语言特点

英文报刊标题的作用类似于广告，它要向读者“推销”文章，激发读者兴趣。新闻刊物的标题常常体现编者和记者的语言素养和文字技巧，进而体现该刊物的质量。研究一下标题语言和其简化现象，无疑对阅读英文报刊具有很大的帮助作用。

报刊英语属于新闻体英语，它有自己的语言特色，尤其反映在标题上。标题是新闻报道内容的集中和概括，是新闻报道的点睛之笔，通常以鲜明的黑体大字在文章的抢眼处标出，它既要扣住全文要点，突出中心，又要新颖醒目，其作用不可忽视。标题用简洁的文字浓缩了新闻中最主要、最值得注意的内容，是新闻英语中很重要的组成部分，常被比喻成“新闻报道的眼睛”，起着“向导”的作用。标题用语短而精，通常只用三言两语或寥寥数字即可表达全文主题。英文报刊标题语言一般具有以下特点：

(1) 词汇简化

英语报刊标题有一些特定的语言体系，总体来讲，每个标题属于一个句法结构，但它又不同于句子，在新闻英语体中称为“标题语言”，有的语言学家称报刊标题所用的词语为“特别词语”或“怪异词语”。标题一般将虚词省略，如冠词、介词、连词等。

为了简约的目的，标题中可省去一切可省之词，甚至包括实义词，有时连主语也可省略。当然这些词的省略以不影响或妨碍读者的理解为标准。然而，有些固定词组或搭配中的词不能省略，如果省略，表示的意思就会不一样。

(2) 语态简化

由于新闻采访方面的原因，英语新闻标题特别常用被动语态。为了简约，be或者 by 通常被省略，以免引出动作执行者。

(3) 时态简化

英语新闻标题中常用的时态主要有一般现在时、一般将来时和现在进行时。一般来说，标题中不用过去时态，通常采用现在时。这种“新闻现在时”很像文学中的“历史现在时”，读者犹如置身其中，不致产生消息已陈旧乏味的感觉。

(4) 标点符号的使用

英语新闻标题只使用部分标点符号，以符代词，紧缩句式，进一步节省字数。一般来说，报刊标题通常不使用标点符号，只是在显示成分关系、表达态度语气时才使用。

(5) 简短小词的使用

英语标题中使用最广泛的是名词和简短小词或单音节短词，这样不但可节省、美化版面，还可增强新闻的简洁性和可读性。这些词多为本族词，具有全民性，通俗易懂。有的语言学家称，过度使用非常短小的词是标题语言的突出特点。这些小词均为带有新闻体特色的词汇，并且词义范畴很宽，新闻英语称这类词为“万能同义词”。有时使用一个这样的词可以表达一个句子，这在新闻英语中称为单词式标题。

(6) 缩写词和节略词的使用

为了节省篇幅，标题中很爱使用缩写词和节略词。缩写词就是几个词的首字母加在一起形成一个词，这在目前人们交际中广泛使用，特别是现在人们的生活节奏不断加快，有人把它们叫做“国际性词汇”或“大众词汇”。这类词在英语新闻报刊标题中亦常常使用。

标题中还经常使用节略词。节略词就是采用“掐头去尾”的方法将一些常用词缩短。目前还出现一些词组节略形式。由于语言精练的需要，英语新闻标题中使用这类节略词组的频率更高。

3 新闻报道的首段

新闻报道的首段非常重要，应该重视新闻报道首段的阅读。英文报刊的新闻报道和中文报刊一样，都在真实的原则下，力求简洁生动，有吸引力，能快而准地给读者提供信息，传达时事。为此，作者往往开门见山，将一则消息的主要内容浓缩在第一段里，使读者一看就能略知此新闻记载了何人(who)，何事(what)，何时(when)，何处(where)，为何原因(why) 以及如何发生(how) 这几大要素，从而对整个事件有一个初步的了解，文章的其余段落都是第一段的延伸和扩展，若无暇阅读，只要浏览第一段便可掌握事件的轮廓。所以，新闻报道的第一段可以说是全文的精华和缩影，必须重视该段的阅读。

4 经济新闻的语言特点

(1) 遣词造句

英文经济新闻一方面体现了新闻报道的时效性、客观性，另一方面又具有很强的专业性，其语言运用有一定的特点和规律，熟悉了解这些语言特征有助于读者更及时、更有效地获取有关的财经信息。

财经报道的主要功能是传递信息。及时了解、准确掌握英文财经报道的信息内容，除需具备一定的专业知识外，还应该对这类报道的语言运用规律和特征有所认识。总体而言，英文财经报道从个别字词的选用到全篇内容的陈述都体现了新闻报道惯有的及时、客观、新颖的特点。另外，由于专业上的需求，财经报道在形式和内容两方面又表现出自己独有的特征。

英文财经报道属于一种专业性的新闻报道，因此，其语言运用的最大特征就是专业名词和专业术语多，而且许多常用词被赋予特殊的含义。如果不了解这些词在专业上的含义，就可能无法真正彻底读懂有关的报道和消息。同时，英文财经报道为了体现新颖、通俗，也经常用一些外来语、俗俚语、口语表达形式以及比较生动、灵活的小词。

财经报道用词的另一个突出特点是形容经济数据及市场变动的词通俗、形象，形容价格走势的动词十分丰富，下面是一些报道中常见的表示“上升”和“下降”的动词：

表示“上升”的动词	表示“下降”的动词
rise 上升	fall 下降
jump 跳升	drop 下落
skyrocket 暴涨	dump 狂泻
surge 急涨	plunge 猛跌
soar 剧增	retreat 回落
climb 攀升	dive 下跌
spurt 突升	tumble 急落
advance 上涨	decline 下降
inch up 缓升	slip 下滑
notch up 升高	shed 跌落
fly 飞升	dip 下降
rebound 反弹	roll back 回落
gain 增长	lose 降低

(2) 句法结构

为了突出新闻报道的及时性和全面性，记者需要在尽量短的时间内发出尽量多的消息。由于没有太多的时间进行语言上的推敲，所以英文财经报道中的句子偏长，结构比较松散，插入成分也通常比较多，比如同位语、插入语及定语从句等。这些成分都是为了补充说明相关的情况和消息。

其次，由于发稿时间紧迫，临时插入的从句省略了连接词，显得与主句的关系不够紧凑。呈现出较强的口语化特点。

另外，财经报道经常涉及各类经济数据、市场价格及其他有关的统计数字，这些数据之间的比较或参照是财经报道的重要组成部分。因此，比较结构在英文财经报道的句型中占有很大的比例。例如，以less/higher/lower/narrower/smaller 等进行比较；以 highest /record high/ lowest 等连接的最高级比较；以 against /opposite/ compare/ contrast 等词进行数据对比等等。

(3) 篇章结构

与普通新闻报道的结构一样，英文财经报道也通常由三部分组成，即标题(Headline)、导语(Lead)和正文(Body)。

标题以一种类似电报体的语言形式，十分简洁地告诉读者所发生的主要事件及有关消息。正文则进一步阐述、说明事件发生的来龙去脉，并提供一些必要的背景材料或知识。为达到客观真实的效果，英文财经报道的正文中往往采用大量的引述。因此，一篇报道中援引政府官员、市场人士、分析评论专家的话层出不穷。引述可以是一段完整的话，或者一句话中的一部分，甚至是原话中一两个词，这属于直接引述。此外，英文财经报道的正文中还有更多的间接引述。这类引述通常以一些常用的表达法引导，如 say(说)，express(表示)，tell(告诉)，according to ...(根据……)等等。所有这些引述都旨在体现报道的客观性和真实性。

5 英文报刊常见栏目名称

Ad/Advertisement 广告
Agony Column 答读者问专栏；私事广告专栏
Anecdote 趣闻轶事
Around Nation 国内新闻
Around The Country 国内新闻版
Around The World 国际新闻版
Back Grounding 新闻背景
Blurb 商品信息
Book Page 书评专页
Book Review 书评
Books 书评
Brief 简讯；简明新闻
Briefing 简报
Budget 要闻索引
Bulletin 新闻简报
Business/Trade 商业 / 贸易
Business 商业版
Campus Life 校园生活
Candid Camera 抓拍镜头；有照为凭
Caricature 漫画；讽刺画
Cartoon 漫画
Chitchat Column 闲话栏
City 本市新闻版

City Edition 本埠新闻版;地方新闻版
City Page 金融和商业新闻版
Classified Ads/ Advertising 分类广告
Column 专栏;栏目
Comic Strip 连环画
Continued Story 连载故事
Correspondence Column 读者来信栏
Cover Story (杂志) 封面报道
Critique 评论
Crossword 猜字游戏;纵横填字字谜
Culture/Science 文化/科技
Digest 文摘
document 文件摘要
Domestic 国内新闻
Domestic News 国内新闻
Double Dayoff Supplement 双休特刊
Economics And Business 经贸版
Editor's Note 编者按
Editorial Page/Editorials 社论版;言论版

6 报刊英语中的常用词汇及短语

accredited journalist 特派记者
advertisement 广告
advance 预发消息;预写消息
affair 桃色新闻;绯闻
anecdote 趣闻轶事
assignment 采写任务
attribution 消息出处;消息来源
back alley news 小道消息
back grounding 新闻背景
Bad news travels quickly. 坏事传千里
Banner 通栏标题
Beat 采写范围
Body 新闻正文
Boil 压缩(篇幅)
box 花边新闻
brief 简讯
bulletin 新闻简报
byline 署名文章
caption 图片说明
caricature 漫画
carry 刊登
cartoon 漫画
censor 审查(新闻稿件),新闻审查
chart (每周流行音乐等) 排行榜
clipping 剪报
column 专栏;栏目
columnist 专栏作家
continued story 连载故事,连载小说
contributing editor 特约编辑
contribution (投给报刊的) 稿件;投稿
contributor 投稿人
copy desk 新闻编辑部
copy editor 文字编辑
correction 更正(启事)
correspondence column 读者来信专栏
correspondent 驻外记者;常驻外埠记者
cover 采访;采写
cover girl 封面女郎
covert coverage 隐性采访;秘密采访
crop 剪辑(图片)

crusade 宣传攻势
cut 插图;删减(字数)
cut line 插图说明
daily 日报
dateline 新闻电头
deadline 截稿时间
dig 深入采访;追踪(新闻线索);挖新闻
digest 文摘
editorial 社论
editorial office 编辑部
editor's notes 编者按
exclusive 独家新闻
expose 揭丑新闻;新闻曝光
extra 号外
eye-account 目击记;记者见闻
faxed photo 传真照片
feature 特写;专稿
feedback 信息反馈
file 发送消息;发稿
filler 补白
First Amendment(美国宪法)第一修正案
five "Ws" of news 新闻五要素
flag 报头;报名
folo (= follow-up) 连续报道
Fourth Estate 第四等级(新闻界的别称)
freedom of the Press 新闻自由
free-lancer 自由撰稿人
full position 醒目位置
Good news comes on crutches. 好事不出门。
Grapevine 小道消息
Gutter 中缝
hard news 硬新闻;纯消息
headline 新闻标题;内容提要
hearsay 小道消息
highlights 要闻
hot news 热点新闻
human interest 人情味
in-depth reporting 深度报道
insert 插补段落;插稿
interpretative reporting 解释性报道
invasion of privacy 侵犯隐私(权)
inverted pyramid 倒金字塔(写作结构)
investigative reporting 调查性报道
journalism 新闻业;新闻学
journalist 新闻记者
kill 退弃(稿件);枪毙(稿件)
layout 版面编排;版面设计
lead 导语
libel 诽谤(罪)
makeup 版面设计
man of the year 年度新闻人物、风云人物
mass communication 大众传播(学)
mass media 大众传播媒介
master head 报头;报名
media 媒介;媒体
morgue 报刊资料室
news agency 通讯社
news clue 新闻线索
news peg 新闻线索;新闻电头

newsprint 新闻纸
news value 新闻价值
nose for news 新闻敏感
obituary 讣告
objectivity 客观性
off the record 不宜公开报道
opinion poll 民意测验
periodical 期刊
pipeline 匿名消息来源
popular paper 大众化报纸；通俗报纸
press 报界；新闻界
press conference 新闻发布会；记者招待会
press law 新闻法
press release 新闻公告；新闻简报
PR man 公关先生
Profile 人物专访；人物特写
Proofreader 校对员
pseudo event 假新闻
quality paper 高级报纸；严肃报纸
quarterly 季刊
readability 可读性
reader's interest 读者兴趣
reject 退弃(稿件)
remuneration 稿费；稿酬
reporter 记者
rewrite 改写(稿件)；改稿
round-up 综合消息
scandal 丑闻
scoop “抢”(新闻)；独家新闻
sensational 耸人听闻的；具有轰动效应的
sex scandal 桃色新闻
sidebar 花絮新闻
slant 主观报道；片面报道
slink ink “爬格子”
soft news 软新闻
source 新闻来源；消息灵通人士
spike 退弃(稿件)；“枪毙”(稿件)
stone 拼版
story 消息；稿件；文章
stringer 特约记者；通讯员
subhead 小标题；副标题
supplement 号外；副刊；增刊
suspended interest 悬念
thumbnail “豆腐块”(文章)
timeliness 时效性；时新性
tip 内幕新闻；秘密消息
trim 删改(稿件)
update 更新(新闻内容)；增强(时效性)
watchdog 舆论监督
weekly 周报
wire service 通讯社

7 世界主要国际通讯社

Associated Press(AP) 美联社(美国)
United Press International(UPI) 合众国际社(美国)
Reuters 路透社(英国)
Agence France Press 法新社(法国)
ITAR-TASS 俄通社(俄罗斯)

Xinhua News Agency 新华社(中国)
ANSA 安莎通讯社(意大利)
Efe 埃菲社(西班牙)
DPA 德意志新闻社(德国)
JIJI 时事通讯社(日本)
KYODO 共同社(日本)
PTI 印报社(印度)
MENA 中东通讯社(埃及)

3 普利策奖

普利策奖也称为普利策新闻奖。1917 年根据美国报业巨头约瑟夫·普利策(Joseph Pulitzer) 的遗愿设立,20 世纪七八十年代已经发展成为美国新闻界的一项最高荣誉奖,每年颁发一次。现在,不断完善的评选制度已使普利策奖成为全球性的一个奖项。

普利策奖在每年的春季由哥伦比亚大学的普利策奖评选委员会的 14 名会员评定,5 月由哥伦比亚大学校长正式颁发。

普利策奖分为两类,新闻界和创作界。新闻界的获奖者可以是任何国籍,但是获奖条目必须在美国周报(或日报)中发表。创作界的获得者必须是美国公民,唯一例外是历史奖。只要是关于美国历史的书都可获奖,作者不必是美国人。

普利策奖的评委由有成就的著名记者组成。当年的优胜者由评委审查、挑选,但评选结果需经哥伦比亚大学顾问委员会通过,并由哥伦比亚大学校长宣布。

首届普利策摄影奖是 1942 年颁发的。此后,除 1946 年外,每年颁发一次。从 1968 年开始,摄影类增设了专题新闻摄影奖,获奖作品通常由一组照片组成。

普利策摄影奖获奖作品具有重要意义。不少美国人对于许多重大事件的深刻印象是由当年普利策奖获奖照片形成的。

普利策奖象征了美国最负责任的写作和最优美的文字,历来被美国作家视为一种荣誉。特别是新闻奖,更是美国报界的最高荣誉。每一个希望有所作为的美国记者无不以获得普利策新闻奖作为奋斗的目标。

参考文献

[1] 郝雁南. 透视文章标题,掌握新闻精髓. 21 世纪报,2005 年 9 月 15 日
[2] 正保外语教学网

附录　外刊网址

美国

http://www.nytimes.com/ 纽约时报
http://www.washingtonpost.com/ 华盛顿邮报
http://www.latimes.com/ 洛杉矶时报
http://online.wsj.com/public/us 华尔街日报
http://chinese.wsj.com/gb/index.asp 华尔街日报中文版
http://www.usatoday.com/ 今日美国
http://www.chicagotribune.com/ 芝加哥论坛报
http://www.nydailynews.com/ 纽约每日新闻
http://www.nypost.com/ 纽约邮报
http://www.csmonitor.com/ 基督教科学箴言报
http://www.iht.com/ 国际先驱论坛报
http://www.newsday.com/ 华盛顿新闻报
http://www.baltimoresun.com/ 巴尔的摩太阳报
http://www.newsweek.com/ 新闻周刊
http://www.businessweek.com/ 商业周刊
http://www.newsweek.com/ 新闻周刊
http://www.time.com/time/ 时代
http://money.cnn.com/magazines/fortune/ 财富
http://www.forbes.com/ 福布斯
http://www.nationalgeographic.com/ 国家地理
http://www.rd.com/ 读者文摘
http://www.life.com/Life/ 生活
http://www.examiner.com/ 旧金山晚报
http://www.chron.com/ 休斯敦时报
http://www.businesstimes.com.sg/ 商业时报

英国

http://www.timesonline.co.uk/tol/news/ 泰晤士报
http://www.ft.com/home/uk 金融时报
http://www.ftchinese.com/index.php 金融时报中文版
http://www.guardian.co.uk/ 卫报
http://www.mirror.co.uk/ 每日镜报
http://www.express.co.uk/home 每日快报
http://observer.guardian.co.uk/ 观察家报
http://www.newsoftheworld.co.uk/ 世界新闻报
http://www.economist.com/ 经济学家
http://www.spectator.co.uk/ 旁观者
http://www.newstatesman.com/ 新政治家
http://www.ipcmedia.com/ 妇女界
http://dsc.discovery.com/ 发现
http://www.nature.com/ 自然
http://www.private-eye.co.uk/ 侦探
http://www.timeout.com/london/ 闲暇
http://www.scotsman.com/ 苏格兰人报

法国

http://www.lefigaro.fr/ 费加罗报
http://www.lemonde.fr/ 世界报
http://www.liberation.fr/ 解放报

新加坡

http://www.zaobao.com/ 联合早报中文版

马来西亚

http://thestar.com.my/ 星报
http://www.intimes.com.my/ 国际时报

泰国

http://www.bangkokpost.net/ 曼谷邮报